Bola Agbaje

Belong

Methuen Drama

Published by Methuen Drama 2012

1 3 5 7 9 10 8 6 4 2

Methuen Drama
Bloomsbury Publishing Plc
50 Bedford Square
London WC1B 3DP
www.methuendrama.com

ISBN: 978 1 408 17283 4

A CIP catalogue record for this book is available from
the British Library

Typeset by Country Setting, Kingsdown, Kent
Printed and bound in Great Britain by
CPI Group (UK) Ltd, Croydon, CR0 4YY

ROYAL COURT

The Royal Court Theatre & Tiata Fahodzi present

BELONG

by **Bola Agbaje**

Belong was first performed at The Royal Court Jerwood Theatre Upstairs, Sloane Square, on Thursday 26th April 2012.

Belong is an original Tiata Fahodzi commission.

Principal Sponsor

Coutts

BELONG

by Bola Agbaje

Kayode **Lucian Msamati**
Rita **Noma Dumezweni**
Fola **Jocelyn Jee Esien**
Kunle **Ashley Zhangazha**
Mama **Pamela Nomvete**
Barman/Buchi/Police Commissioner **Itoya Osagiede**
Chief Olowolaye **Richard Pepple**

Director **Indhu Rubasingham**
Designer **Ben Stones**
Lighting Designer **Malcolm Rippeth**
Sound Designer **David McSeveney**
Casting Director **Amy Ball**
Assistant Director **Titas Halder**
Production Manager **Tariq Rifaat**
Stage Managers **Sarah Alford-Smith & Mary O'Hanlon**
Stage Management Work Placement **George Cook**
Costume Supervisors **Claire Wardroper & Iona Kenrick**
Fight Director **Bret Yount**
Set Builders **Footprint Scenery Ltd.**
Scenic Painter **Jodie Pritchard**

The Royal Court, Tiata Fahodzi and Stage Management wish to thank the following for their help with this production: Femi Elufowoju, jr for commissioning Belong for Tiata Fahodzi and initial dramaturgy, Emily McLaughlin for dramaturgy, Bang and Olufsen, Alex MacColl at MacKing, Booker, Johan Persson, The Entryphone Company Ltd. and Olabisi Agbaje.

THE COMPANY

BOLA AGBAJE (Writer)

Bola was a member of the Young Writers' Programme at the Royal Court Theatre, and her first play, Gone Too Far!, premiered in the Jerwood Theatre Upstairs at the Royal Court in 2007, directed by Bijan Sheibani, and then transferred Downstairs for a sell out run in 2008.

FOR THE ROYAL COURT: Off The Endz, Gone Too Far!, Sorry Seems To Be the Hardest Word (Latitude).

OTHER THEATRE INCLUDES: Three Blind Mice (Cardboard Citizens); Playing The Game, Detaining Justice (Tricycle); My Territory, Anything You Can Do (Soho); Legend Of Moremi (Tiata Fahodzi, for the Tenth Anniversary Gala at Theatre Royal Stratford East); Good Neighbours, Reap What You Sow (Young Vic); In Time (Tiata Fahodzi at the Almeida and on tour with Eastern Angles); Rivers Run Deep (Hampstead).

AWARDS INCLUDE: 2008 Olivier Award for Outstanding Achievement in an Affiliated Theatre for Gone Too Far!

Bola is currently under under commission to 20 Stories High and Ludere Productions. She is also developing Gone Too Far! into a screenplay with Poission Rouge Pictures and the BFI.

NOMA DUMEZWENI (Rita)

FOR THE ROYAL COURT: Dream in the Wasteland.

OTHER THEATRE INCLUDES: A Walk on Part (Soho); Adelaide Road, The Winter's Tale, Julius Caesar, The Grainstore, Morte D'Arthur, Romeo and Juliet, Little Eagles, Macbeth, Breakfast With Mugabe, Anthony & Cleopatra, Much Ado About Nothing (RSC); Six Characters in Search of an Author (Chichester/West End); The Hour We Knew Nothing of Each Other, President of an Empty Room (National); A Raisin in the Sun (Young Vic at the Lyric Hammersmith/UK Tour); A Midsummer Night's Dream, The Master and Margarita, Nathan the Wise, The Coffee House (Chichester), Skellig, The Blacks (Young Vic); Ali Baba and the Forty Thieves, A Midsummer Night's Dream (London Bubble); The Bogus Woman (Red Room/Bush); Know Your Rights (Red Room/BAC).

TELEVISION INCLUDES: Casualty, Doctor Who, Summerhill, Eastenders, The Last Enemy, The Grey Man, New Tricks, Shameless, Holby City, Little Miss Jocelyn, Silent Witness, People Like Us, The Knock, Fallout, After Thomas, Together, The Colour of Magic, Fallen Angel.

FILM INCLUDES: Magpie Sings the Blues, Daniel Cares, Dirty Pretty Things, Rugby Road, Macbeth, The Escort.

RADIO INCLUDES: The No. 1 Ladies Detective Agency, The Mother in Law's Assassin, Pilgrim, A Time for Justice, The Farming of Bones, From Freedom to the Future, From Fact to Fiction, Sagila, Shylock, Handprint, Last Minute Grooming, Geronimo, Taxi, Far and Beyond, Nathan the Wise, Back Home, The Bogus Woman, The Interpreter.

AWARDS INCLUDE: 2006 Olivier Award for Best Supporting Performer for A Raisin in the Sun; Fringe First & Manchester Evening News Award for The Bogus Woman.

JOCELYN JEE ESIEN (Fola)

FOR THE ROYAL COURT: The Lion and the Jewel.

OTHER THEATRE INCLUDES: Bonded, Tickets and Ties (Tiata Fahodzi); One Monkey Don't Stop No Show (Eclipse/Sheffield Theatres); Vagina Monologues (Mark Goucher Ltd); Racing Demon (Chichester/Toronto Tour); Torn (Arcola).

LIVE COMEDY INCLUDES: Smirnoff Festival Tour (South Africa), Lucky Strike Tour (Holland); Sprite International Comedy Tour (South Africa); Richard Blackwood Tour; Edinburgh Festival.

TELEVISION INCLUDES: The Sarah Jane Adventures, Uncle Max – Series 2, Little Miss Jocelyn – Series 1 & 2, Holby City, Musical Chairs, The Lenny Henry Show – Series 1 & 2, 3 Non Blondes – Series 1 & 2, Ed Stone Is Dead, In the Name of Love, Comedy Nation, The Fast Show, Douglas, The Bill, Collision, Stop the World, Comedy Shuffle, Blouse and Skirt, The 291 Show at the Hackney Empire, The Warehouse, Jim Davidson Presents, 28 Acts in 28 Minutes, Saturday Live Again, Strictly Confidential, 1 Non Blonde: Down Under, Some Girls.

FILM INCLUDES: Anuvahood, Baby Mother, Street Dance, Bridget Jones' Diary.

RADIO INCLUDES: Beauty of Britain, Comedy Comes Home, Jocelyn Jees Up, Towers of Babel.

AWARDS INCLUDE: Screen Nation Award for Best Comedy for 3 Non Blondes; Black Entertainment Award for 3 Non Blondes and Little Miss Jocelyn; Best Newcomer at the Women in Film and Television Awards for Little Miss Jocelyn; Afro Hollywood Award for Little Miss Jocelyn; Best Actress at the Music, Video and Screen Awards; Comedy Store Hooch Award for Stand Up, Best Actress and Best Comedy at the Merit of Honour Awards.

TITAS HALDER (Assistant Director)

AS A DIRECTOR, THEATRE INCLUDES: The Goat at Midnight (Bush); Write to Rock (Clwyd Theatr, Cymru); Painting a Wall (Finborough).
AS ASSISTANT/ASSOCIATE DIRECTOR, THEATRE INCLUDES: King Lear (Donmar/UK Tour/BAM); Passion, The Prince of Homburg, The Late Middle Classes, Polar Bears (Donmar), Stones In His Pockets (Tricycle/Belfast Opera House); The Roundabout Season (Paines Plough/Sheffield Crucible); Stovepipe (High Tide/National/Bush).
Titas is also a playwright and trained on the Royal Court Theatre Young Writers' Programme.

LUCIAN MSAMATI (Kayode)

FOR THE ROYAL COURT: Clybourne Park (& West End).
OTHER THEATRE INCLUDES: Comedy of Errors, Death and the King's Horseman, The Overwhelming, President of an Empty Room, Mourning Becomes Electra (National); Ruined, ID (Almeida); The Resistible Rise of Arturo Ui, Firework-Maker's Daughter (Lyric Hammersmith); Pericles (RSC); Fabulation, Gem of the Ocean, Walk Hard (Tricycle); Who Killed Mr Drum? (Riverside Studios); Romeo and Juliet (Dancehouse, Manchester); Taming the Shrew (Bath Shakespeare Fest. Also as Director); Born African (HIFA/BAC/Arthur Seaton Theatre, NY); Twelfth Night (Neus Globe Theatre, Germany/Edinburgh Fest.); Fade to Black (Harare International Festival of the Arts); Eternal Peace Asylum (American Rep.); Loot (Over the Edge Theatre Co.); Urfaust (Zimbabwe-German Society/Over the Edge Theatre Co.); Rocky Horror Show (Seven Arts Theatre).
TELEVISION INCLUDES: Game of Thrones, Richard II, Ashes to Ashes, Dr Who, No 1 Ladies Detective Agency, The Andi O Show, Spooks, Ultimate Force, To Close for Comfort, The Knock.
FILM INCLUDES: The International, Short Cuts, Coffin, Dr Juju, Lumumba.
RADIO INCLUDES: The Jero Plays, The Mugabe Plays, The Virtuous Burglar.
Lucian has also worked extensively as a radio producer and presenter, as well as a copywriter, director and playwright. His writing credits include Houseboy, Memory Play, Zuva Crumbing, Eternal Peace Asylum and Born African.
Lucian Msamati is the Artistic Director of Tiata Fahodzi.

DAVID McSEVENEY (Sound Designer)

David trained at the Central School of Speech and Drama completing a BA Hons. in Theatre Practice (Sound Design).

FOR THE ROYAL COURT: Vera Vera Vera, Constellations, The Village Bike, Clybourne Park (& West End), Ingredient X, Posh, Disconnect, Cock, A Miracle, The Stone, Shades, Seven Jewish Children, The Girlfriend Experience (& Theatre Royal Plymouth & Young Vic), Contractions, Fear & Misery/War & Peace.

OTHER THEATRE INCLUDES: Stones in His Pockets (Tricycle); Victoria Station/One for the Road (Print Room & Young Vic); On The Record (Arcola); The Tin Horizon (Theatre503); Gaslight (Old Vic); Charley's Aunt, An Hour and a Half Late (Theatre Royal Bath); A Passage to India, After Mrs Rochester, Madame Bovary (Shared Experience); Men Should Weep, Rookery Nook (Oxford Stage Company); Othello (Southwark Playhouse).

AS ASSISTANT DESIGNER: The Permanent Way (Out of Joint); My Brilliant Divorce, Auntie and Me (West End); Accidental Death of an Anarchist (Donmar).

David is Head of Sound at the Royal Court.

PAMELA NOMVETE (Mama)

FOR THE ROYAL COURT: truth & reconciliation, Now or Later, Marching for Fausa, Leavetaking.

OTHER THEATRE INCLUDES: The Comedy of Errors, Welcome to Thebes, Racing Daemon, The David Hare Trilogy, Fuente Ovejuna (National); The Archbishop and the Antichrist (Soho); Twelfth Night (RSC/West End); Talking in Tounges (Lyric Hammersmith); Sanctuary (Joint Stock); Raisin in the Sun (Durban Playhouse); The Woman of Sharkville, Nothing But the Truth (Market Theatre, South Africa); Going to St Ives (Peter Turin Theatre, South Africa); Salvation (South Africa National Tour).

TELEVISION INCLUDES: Lewis, Sometimes in April, Behind the Badge, Generations, Born Free: A New Adventure, Eastenders.

FILM INCLUDES: The Special Relationship, Zulu Love Letter, A Reasonable Man, Human Time Bomb, Orion's Key.

AWARDS INCLUDE: 1995 Best Actress Award for Raisin in the Sun; 1999/2000 Duku Duku Award for Best Actress for Generations; Fespaco Film Award for Best Actress for Zulu Love Letter; 2003 Naledi Award for Best Actress Award for Nothing But the Truth.

ITOYA OSAGIEDE (Barman / Buchi / Police Commissioner)

This is Itoya's professional stage debut.

RICHARD PEPPLE (Chief Olowolaye)

THEATRE INCLUDES: The Rise and Shine of Comrade Fiasco, Memory Play, Tiata Tamba Tamba, 365 Plays/365 Days, The Estate, The Burial (Tiata Fahodzi); Fixer, Full Circle (Oval House); The Garbage King (Unicorn); High Life (Hampstead); Medea Medea (Headlong/Gate); The Hounding of David Oluwale (Eclipse/West Yorkshire Playhouse); White Open Spaces (Pentabus); Coriolanus (RSC); The Estate (Soho/Tiata Fahodzi); In The Blood (Finborough).

TELEVISION INCLUDES: Caught in a Trap, Shoot the Messenger, The Bill, Nathan Barley.

FILM INCLUDES: No Ordinary Trifle, Pussyfooting.

RADIO INCLUDES: The Spy, The Man in Black, Why Is the Sky So Blue?, The Prison Graduates, Power Failure, Next of Kin, A Second Night to Midnight, Revenge of the Celebrity Mums, The Estate.

MALCOLM RIPPETH (Lighting Designer)

FOR THE ROYAL COURT: The Acid Test, Kin, Spur of the Moment.

OTHER THEATRE INCLUDES: The Umbrellas of Cherbourg, Six Characters in Search of an Author (West End); Brief Encounter (Kneehigh – West End/Broadway); The Wild Bride, The Red Shoes (Kneehigh); Stones in His Pockets (Tricycle); Decade, Faustus (Headlong); The Lady from the Sea (Rose Theatre); HMS Pinafore (Guthrie, Minneapolis); Calendar Girls (West End/Australia/Canada); The Pitchfork Disney (Arcola); Little Women (Gate Theatre, Dublin); The Seven Year Itch (Salisbury Playhouse); A Very Old Man with Enormous Wings (Little Angel); His Dark Materials (Birmingham Rep); The Field (Dublin); The Devil Inside Him (National Theatre Wales).

OPERA INCLUDES: Armida (Garsington); Seven Deadly Sins (WNO).

DANCE INCLUDES: Designer Body, La Nuit Intime (balletLORENT).

AWARDS INCLUDE: 2010 OBIE for Brief Encounter in New York; 2009 Theatregoers' Choice Award for Best Lighting Designer for Brief Encounter and Six Characters in Search of an Author.

INDHU RUBASINGHAM (Director)

FOR THE ROYAL COURT: Disconnect, Free Outgoing, Lift Off, Clubland, The Crutch & Sugar Mummies.

OTHER THEATRE INCLUDES: Ruined (Almeida); Stones In His Pockets, Fabulation, Starstruck, Women Power & Politics (Tricycle); The Great Game: Afghanistan (Tricycle/USA Tour); Wuthering Heights (Birmingham Rep/UK Tour); Yellowman, Anna in the Tropic (Hampstead); The Waiting Room (National); Ramayana (National/Birmingham Rep); The Misanthrope, Secret Rapture, Romeo and Juliet (Chichester); Pure Gold (Soho); Heartbreak House (Watford Palace); Sugar Dollies, Shakuntala (Gate); No Boys Cricket, Club, Gulp Fiction, D'Yer Eat With Yer Fingers?!, Party Girls (Theatre Royal, Stratford East); A Time of Fire, Kaahini (Birmingham Rep); Yellowman, The Morris (Liverpool Everyman); A River Sutra (Three Milllsland Studios); A Dolls House (Young Vic).

OPERA INCLUDES: Another America (Almeida/Sadler's Wells).

Indhu is currently the Artistic Director of the Tricycle Theatre, and has previously been Associate Director for the Gate Theatre, Birmingham Rep and the Young Vic.

BEN STONES (Designer)

Ben trained in stage design at Central Saint Martin's College of Art.

FOR THE ROYAL COURT: Ingredient X.

OTHER THEATRE INCLUDES: Creditors (Donmar/BAM, New York); Kiss Of The Spider Woman (Donmar); Lower Ninth (Donmar West End); An Enemy of the People, My Dads a Birdman (Sheffield Crucible); Beautiful Thing (Sound Theatre); Paradise Lost (Headlong); The Arab Israeli Cookbook (Tricycle); The Mighty Boosh, Mitchell and Webb Live! (UK Tour); When Five Years Pass (Arcola); Speaking in Tongues (West End); The Lady In The Van (National); The Herbal Bed, The Real Thing (Salisbury Playhouse); Romeo and Juliet (Globe); Encourage the Others (Almeida); Doctor Faustus, Edward II, Taste of Honey, Salt (Royal Exchange, Manchester); No Idea (Young Vic); The Painter (Arcola); Da (Gate Theatre, Dublin); Some Like It Hip Hop (Sadlers Wells/UK Tour); The Kitchen Sink (Bush); Paul Merton Live (UK Tour).

TELEVISION INCLUDES: Crocodile (a new play by Frank McGuinness).

AWARDS INCLUDE: 2011 MEN award for Best Design for Doctor Faustus at the Royal Exchange, Manchester.

ASHLEY ZHANGAZHA (Kunle)

FOR THE ROYAL COURT: truth and reconciliation.

OTHER THEATRE INCLUDES: Richard II, King Lear (Donmar); Danton's Death (National); Oliver!, Whistle Down the Wind, Hey Mr Producer (West End).

TELEVISION INCLUDES: Lenny Goes to Town.

tiata fahodzi
africans in british theatre

'Tiata Fahodzi' amalgamates Yoruba (Nigeria) and Twi (Ghana) and means 'theatre of the emancipated.'

The company was founded in 1997 by Femi Elufowoju, jr to explore the living experiences of Africans in Britain. Tiata Fahodzi has produced classics of African theatre alongside new commissions from leading and emerging writers. Its Tiata Delights festivals have proved highly successful in showcasing new plays which are subsequently taken up by other producers. In 2009, Oladipo Agboluaje's Iya-Ile, staged in partnership with Soho Theatre, was another huge hit with audiences and critics and earned an Olivier Award nomination.

Tiata Fahodzi is delighted to be working with the Royal Court to create Belong. Bola Agbaje was inspired to write for the stage by seeing Tiata Fahodzi's 2005 production of Ola Rotimi's The Gods are Not to Blame at Arcola Theatre.

Under the Artistic Directorship of Lucian Msamati, Tiata Fahodzi is embarking on Tiata Tamba Tamba (from Shona: 'play play!'), a major programme centred on emancipating the creativity of the actor.

Projects in development include:
The Epic Adventure of Nhamo the Manyika Warrior and His Sexy Wife Chipo by Denton Chikura
Houseboy by Lucian Msamati, adapted from the classic novel by Ferdinand Oyono

Oladipo Agboluaje is commissioned to write the final part of the trilogy of plays which began with The Estate and Iya-Ile.

Tiata Fahodzi is an Associate Company of Soho Theatre and is an Arts Council of England National Portfolio Organisation.

THE ENGLISH STAGE COMPANY
AT THE ROYAL COURT THEATRE

'For me the theatre is really a religion or way of life. You must decide what you feel the world is about and what you want to say about it, so that everything in the theatre you work in is saying the same thing ... A theatre must have a recognisable attitude. It will have one, whether you like it or not.'

George Devine, first artistic director of the English Stage Company: notes for an unwritten book.

photo: Stephen Cummiskey

As Britain's leading national company dedicated to new work, the Royal Court Theatre produces new plays of the highest quality, working with writers from all backgrounds, and addressing the problems and possibilities of our time.

"The Royal Court has been at the centre of British cultural life for the past 50 years, an engine room for new writing and constantly transforming the theatrical culture." Stephen Daldry

Since its foundation in 1956, the Royal Court has presented premieres by almost every leading contemporary British playwright, from John Osborne's Look Back in Anger to Caryl Churchill's A Number and Tom Stoppard's Rock 'n' Roll. Just some of the other writers to have chosen the Royal Court to premiere their work include Edward Albee, John Arden, Richard Bean, Samuel Beckett, Edward Bond, Leo Butler, Jez Butterworth, Martin Crimp, Ariel Dorfman, Stella Feehily, Christopher Hampton, David Hare, Eugène Ionesco, Ann Jellicoe, Terry Johnson, Sarah Kane, David Mamet, Martin McDonagh, Conor McPherson, Joe Penhall, Lucy Prebble, Mark Ravenhill, Simon Stephens, Wole Soyinka, Polly Stenham, David Storey, Debbie Tucker Green, Arnold Wesker and Roy Williams.

"It is risky to miss a production there." Financial Times

In addition to its full-scale productions, the Royal Court also facilitates international work at a grass roots level, developing exchanges which bring young writers to Britain and sending British writers, actors and directors to work with artists around the world. The research and play development arm of the Royal Court Theatre, The Studio, finds the most exciting and diverse range of new voices in the UK. The Studio runs play-writing groups including the Young Writers Programme, Critical Mass for black, Asian and minority ethnic writers and the biennial Young Writers Festival. For further information, go to www.royalcourttheatre.com/playwriting/the-studio.

"Yes, the Royal Court is on a roll. Yes, Dominic Cooke has just the genius and kick that this venue needs... It's fist-bitingly exciting." Independent

ROYAL COURT SUPPORTERS

The Royal Court is able to offer its unique playwriting and audience development programmes because of significant and longstanding partnerships with the organisations that support it.

Coutts is the Principal Sponsor of the Royal Court. The Genesis Foundation supports the Royal Court's work with International Playwrights. Theatre Local is sponsored by Bloomberg. The Jerwood Charitable Foundation supports new plays by playwrights through the Jerwood New Playwrights series. The Andrew Lloyd Webber Foundation supports the Royal Court's Studio, which aims to seek out, nurture and support emerging playwrights. Over the past ten years the BBC has supported the Gerald Chapman Fund for directors.

The Harold Pinter Playwright's Award is given annually by his widow, Lady Antonia Fraser, to support a new commission at the Royal Court.

PUBLIC FUNDING
Arts Council England, London
British Council
European Commission Representation in the UK

CHARITABLE DONATIONS
American Friends of the Royal Court
Martin Bowley Charitable Trust
Gerald Chapman Fund
City Bridge Trust
Cowley Charitable Trust
The Dorset Foundation
The John Ellerman Foundation
The Eranda Foundation
Genesis Foundation
J Paul Getty Jnr Charitable Trust
The Golden Bottle Trust
The Haberdashers' Company
Paul Hamlyn Foundation
Jerwood Charitable Foundation
Marina Kleinwort Charitable Trust
The Leathersellers' Company
The Andrew Lloyd Webber Foundation
John Lyon's Charity
The Andrew W Mellon Foundation
The David & Elaine Potter Foundation
Rose Foundation
Royal Victoria Hall Foundation
The Dr Mortimer & Theresa Sackler Foundation
John Thaw Foundation
The Vandervell Foundation
The Garfield Weston Foundation

CORPORATE SUPPORTERS & SPONSORS
BBC
Bloomberg
Coutts
Ecosse Films
Kudos Film & Television
MAC
Moët & Chandon
Oakley Capital Limited
Smythson of Bond Street
White Light Ltd

BUSINESS ASSOCIATES, MEMBERS & BENEFACTORS
Auerbach & Steele Opticians
Bank of America Merrill Lynch
Hugo Boss
Lazard
Louis Vuitton
Oberon Books
Peter Jones
Savills
Vanity Fair

DEVELOPMENT ADVOCATES
John Ayton MBE
Elizabeth Bandeen
Kinvara Balfour
Anthony Burton CBE
Piers Butler
Sindy Caplan
Sarah Chappatte
Cas Donald (Vice Chair)
Celeste Fenichel
Emma Marsh (Chair)
William Russell
Deborah Shaw Marquardt (Vice Chair)
Sian Westerman
Nick Wheeler
Daniel Winterfeldt

Supported by
ARTS COUNCIL ENGLAND

A PLAY BY
LAURA WADE

ROYAL COURT

Acknowledgements

To my family, who have been my inspiration. I wake up chasing my dreams every day because of the belief and unconditional love they have for me. Sikirat Agbaje, Olakunle Agbaje, Olabisi Agbaje, Abiola Agbaje, Ladi Agbaje, Abisola Agbaje, Wendy Adeyanju.

To my family in Nigeria, who have helped with my Yoruba translations and put up with my many questions about Nigeria and its history. Taiye and Kehinde Hamza, Ahmed Mahmood, Toyin Bolanta, Posi Agbaje, Kunmi Agbaje, Ladi Agbaje, Tennie Agbaje.

Giles Smart and Andy Gout.

Dominic Cooke, Emily McLaughlin, Lucian Msamati, Thomas Kell, Femi Elufowoju Jr.

A big thank-you to the cast and crew of *Belong*, Tiata Fahodzi and the staff at the Royal Court Theatre.

Banks Eniola and Kayode Akintemi, for the hours they spent educating me about African politics.

Lastly I would like to acknowledge my friends. Thank you for always being there. Chioma Ishiodu, Charlene Degraft, Nyah Maskell, Chinwe Nwokolo, Ayo Osideinde, Ay Adegboyega, Jennifer Maleghemi, Israel Agbahor and Destiny Ekaragha.

Belong

To all my family in Nigeria

*Each player must accept the cards life deals him or her.
But once they are in hand, he or she alone must decide
how to play the cards in order to win the game.*

Characters

Kayode, *black man, forty-five. Well-spoken, sometimes has a Nigerian accent.*

Rita, *Kayode's wife. Black woman, thirty-five. Nigerian, speaks English.*

Fola, *friend, black woman, forty. Well-spoken with a Nigerian accent.*

Kunle, *black boy, twenty-eight. Nigerian accent.*

Mama, *Kayode's mother, sixty-five. Well-spoken with a Nigerian accent. (Must be able to sing.)*

Barman/Buchi, *black men, early twenties. Strong African accents (may be played by same actor).*

Chief Olowolaye, *Kunle's boss. Black man, fifty. Strong African accent.*

Police Commissioner *(Samson Ali-Amin), black man, forty. African accent.*

The following characters may be voice-overs:
Beggars
Groundnut Trader
Pure Water Trader
Drinks Trader
Passers-by *in the market*

Scene One

England. **Kayode** *and* **Rita***'s living room. It's a beautiful modern flat but it is hard to tell with all the mess. A 'congratulations Kayode' banner and balloons have not been taken down: the banner is hanging off the wall and the deflated balloons are all over the floor. The flat that had been well organised and tidy is now a complete mess. There is rubbish littering the floor. Two empty champagne bottles are on the floor and empty takeaway containers next to them.* **Kayode** *is lying down on the sofa in his pyjamas with a blanket covering him head to toe.*

Silence.

Keys jingle in the door and **Rita** *enters. She is dressed in a designer suit and has on a pair of black shades. She is carrying a takeaway bag and has a bunch of newspapers and letters. She looks around the room and shakes her head. She looks over at* **Kayode** *on the sofa. She walks straight through the room to the bedroom.* **Kayode** *turns over on the sofa.* **Rita** *returns without her suit jacket.*

She throws a bunch of letters towards **Kayode***, which land on the floor. He turns over on the sofa and puts the blanket over his head.* **Rita** *sits on the sofa and starts opening her letters. She rips up each of the bills and puts them in a pile on the floor. She looks over at* **Kayode***.*

Rita   This place is not going to clean itself, Kayode.

Kayode *gets up from the sofa and heads out of the room.*

He exits.

Rita   You think you're the only one who finds it hard dealing with this? (*She shouts back to* **Kayode***.*) You're still a trending topic on Twitter! (*She puts on a different voice.*) Mrs Adetunji, did he really mean those things? (*She puts on another voice.*) Oh you poor thing, you must be . . . blah blah blah blah blah.

She kisses her teeth long and hard for what appears to be ages.

She slumps back on the sofa and closes her eyes. There is a familiar knock on the door and she jumps out of her seat. She heads towards the door and looks through the peephole. The knocking continues.

Rita (*to herself*)   No no, please no.

She tiptoes backwards and starts clearing rubbish from the floor.

Fola (*offstage*)   Hello.

Rita   I'm coming.

She runs to call **Kayode** *from the bedroom.*

Rita   Kayode, Kayode.

The knocking continues.

Fola (*offstage*)   Rita, Kayode, is anyone there? The concierge said to come right up.

Rita *grabs as much rubbish as she can and throws it over the sofa.*

Rita   Give me a minute.

She looks in the mirror next to the door and tidies herself before she opens it. **Fola** *flies in with her suitcases in tow. She drops the bags and gives* **Rita** *a big hug.*

Fola   Oh my dear Rita. It is so terrible what happened. It is by God's grace I was already at the airport when Kayode phoned me.

Rita   He phoned you?

Fola   I just knew from the tone of his voice that he needed a shoulder to cry on, and whose shoulder better than –

Rita   – his wife's!

Fola   You are not one to cope well under pressure.

Rita   Don't worry I am –

Fola   Where is Kayode?

Rita   He's, erm, sleeping . . .

Fola   Ah ah, Rita, look at this place now. You looks like you live in a homeless shelter.

Rita   I was about to start tidying up before . . .

Fola   KAYODE, KAYODE, KAYODE!

Rita   I said he is asleep . . .

Kayode *enters the room. He has changed into a pair of jogging bottoms and a vest.* **Fola** *sees him, runs to him and gives him a hug.*

Fola   Oh, Kayode I am so sorry to hear.

She starts coughing and pushes him away.

Have you drowned yourself in after-shave? Look at you! (*To* **Rita**.) Look at this place.

Kayode *slumps on to the sofa. He picks up his mobile from the floor and starts piecing it together.* **Fola** *starts packing up some of the rubbish on the floor.*

Fola (*to* **Rita**)   Oya Rita, go and get a black bag now. How can you live in a place like this?

Rita   Ask him.

Fola   You are the lady of the house, it is your job to keep the place clean.

Rita   The housekeeper . . .

Fola   Housekeeper? No o.

Rita   Says the woman who has several house girls.

Fola   I'm a busy woman.

Rita   And I'm not?

Fola   Sitting in your boutique all day painting your nails is a luxury. (*To* **Kayode**.) Kayode, why are you wasting money on a housekeeper when you have a perfectly able-bodied woman in the house? (*To* **Rita**.) Please, Rita, get me a bag o. We cannot wait for a stranger to come and tidy up this place for you. Are you not ashamed for your guest to come and see your house in this state?

Rita *heads out of the room.*

Rita   We didn't know we were having any guests.

Kayode   Fola, please sit down.

Fola   I won't be able to sit down in this mess.

Kayode   You just like wahala.

Rita *returns to the room with a Tesco bag.* **Fola** *snatches it out of her hand and begins putting the rubbish in it.* **Rita** *watches as* **Fola** *tidies up.*

Kayode (*to* **Fola**)   Why didn't you call me when you landed? I would have come and picked you up . . .

Fola   I have been ringing your phone.

Rita   You should have called me.

Fola   I know you are a busy woman, I didn't want to disturb you.

She smiles at **Rita**, *who puts on a big fake smile and smiles back.*

Rita   You know you never disturb us when you stay here. (*To herself.*) Only annoy us.

Fola   You are going to need more than one bag for all of this mess. Go and bring me a black bag.

Rita   I can't find one.

Fola   Okay. Just go and bring me more of these small ones. Sometimes you have to make do abi.

Rita *exits and lets out a sigh.* **Fola** *picks up the takeaway containers and places them in the bag.*

Fola (*to* **Kayode**)   Who has been eating all of this nonsense?

Rita *enters the room and hands the bag to* **Fola**. **Fola** *gives her a dirty look and does not take the bag,* **Rita** *takes the hint and starts picking up rubbish from the floor.*

Fola   Rita, why have you not been feeding your husband properly?

Rita   There is food in the fridge.

Fola (*to* **Kayode**)   Don't you want some real food?

Rita It is real food . . .

Fola Eba, amala or pounded yam?

Rita Fola!

Fola I am going to have to go and do some shopping . . .

Rita Fola, stop it!

Fola Stop what? I am just concerned. Your husband is a bag of bones whilst you are just piling on the weight. Getting fatter and fatter every day it seems. So it's only you that is getting the enjoyment from all the takeaway food you eat. You are making your husband suffer. How much weight have you gained since my last visit? I am sure it has to be more than two stones. Look at your fat cheeks and the way your belly is sticking out like there is a baby growing inside . . . or are you pregnant? Is that why you have been slacking at your duties?

Rita I am not pregnant!

Fola Then my sister, please, I beg you. I think you have to join the gym o fast.

Kayode Fola leave her alone.

Fola Nah, truth I dey talk now, Kay. (*To* **Rita**.) It is not right that you are letting yourself go like this. A woman needs to keep her shape for her man.

Rita And where is your man?

Kayode Rita!

Rita She was asking for it.

Kayode That was below the belt.

Rita Didn't you hear what she has been saying about me?

Fola I am only playing with you, Rita. Don't take it too personal. You are becoming too sensitive.

Rita Sorry.

Fola *hugs her.*

Fola   As always, I forgive you, I cannot stay mad at my junior sister now. What is going on with this hair style of yours? You look like a Jamo.

Kayode   Folake, you have just landed, take a seat please. Relax.

Fola *obeys* **Kayode** *and hands her bag to* **Rita** *to continue tidying.*

Fola (*to* **Kayode**)   Tell me what happened now? Why is your face plastered all over the newspaper, telly, internet, YouTube, Twitter, BlackBerry . . .

Rita   He doesn't want to talk . . .

Fola   Of course he wants to talk. Why else would he tell me to come? (*To* **Kayode**.) I cannot believe all of the nonsense I have been hearing.

Rita   Now is not the time . . .

Fola   Kayode, I want to know what happened?

Rita   He will tell you in his own time, but right now . . .

Kayode (*to* **Fola**)   I don't know what came over me.

Rita   Pardon?

Fola   Shh, Rita, he is telling the story.

Kayode   You know me Fola.

Fola   Of course I know you well *well*!

Kayode   I can't tell you why I said it. Why I reacted how –

Fola   So you did say it?

Kayode   Should have stayed off my Twitter page.

Fola   Go on . . .

Kayode   I worked my fingers to the bones. My campaign was watertight . . . 'Can you trust an African?' was the headline! All of a sudden there is this doubt. Why? Cos I'm a frigging African . . . FUCKING BULLSHIT!

Fola (*to* **Kayode**)   I hope you see now what I have been telling you for years. Your Hinglish is better than the Queen's and they still call you . . .

Kayode   Fola! This is my home.

Fola   You fool yourself when you say that you are British.

Rita   Truth be told, people did not have a problem with Kayode or his nationality. (*To* **Kayode**.) You may not like to hear this, babes, but it was your conduct during your campaign.

Kayode   My campaign was flawless!

Rita   Accusing your opponent of being a racist?

Kayode   I spoke the truth.

Rita   He was black!

Kayode   And British!

Rita (*to* **Fola**)   People don't like being told to get off of their 'lazy' arses or being called dumb illiterate monkeys.

Fola   Kayode is right. Oyinbo [*white*] people like to complain too much about –

Rita   It wasn't white people Kayode was talking about. (*To* **Kayode**.) His party's campaign was directed at the black community and they couldn't – (*To* **Fola**.) – relate to him. They thought he was a pompous stuck-up – hate to say it . . . a coconut!

Kayode   Say what you really think.

Rita   The only way you're gonna get over this fall is if you get back up again. There are still people out there rooting for you.

Kayode   To do what exactly?

Rita   Re-strategise. There will be a next time. It's just a minor setback.

Kayode   Not for five years. This isn't where I was meant to be.

Rita   Oh, please.

Kayode   I'm no spring chicken. I have put so much into this campaign and for what? For people to vote for a liar and a cheat. All because his red book was issued at birth and mine at twenty-five. I still can't believe it. This man was fiddling his expenses and was the face of the MP scandal just two years ago . . . and everyone has forgotten!

Rita   And that's good. People will forget this too.

Kayode   I DID NOTHING WRONG, WHY CAN'T YOU GET THAT THROUGH YOUR THICK HEAD! My crime was being a Nigerian. I am being chastised for being an African! No matter how many times I seem to tell you, you don't understand. You just take their side and . . .

Fola   Take it easy, Kay.

Kayode   You don't get it, Rita. I don't know what I am going to do with myself now. (*To* **Fola**.) She does not listen to me. (*To* **Rita**.) I wanted this! I really wanted this. (*To* **Fola**.) I need a break from this place.

Fola   Yes, a break – great idea. Come and work in Nigeria. It will be a new start. Nigeria is flourishing and crying out for people like you . . .

Kayode   No, just a break.

Fola   That place needs Nigerians from the diaspora with skills to help rebuild the country. Forget England, it's crumbling to the ground. Nigeria is on its way up. Jump on board now.

Rita   I am staying right here.

Fola   The way you talk sometimes, people will think you were not even from there . . .

Rita   My life, our life and our future is here.

Fola (*to* **Kayode**)   Do you feel the same?

Rita   Yes, he does.

Kayode (*to* **Rita**)   What's the harm if I take a break?

Rita   We need to talk about this.

Fola   This is exactly what we are doing now.

Rita   Not we, me and Kayode!

Silence.

Rita *stares at* **Fola** *and* **Fola** *stares right back, not taking the hint to leave. She finally gets it and stands up.*

Fola   Of course. I need to go and take a shower again . . . I am all hot and sweaty from all this tidying I have done for this place. The mess is making me itch.

Rita   If you can put the clothes that are on the bed in the corner. I will collect them later. There are some new sheets in the cupboard. I didn't get a chance to make the bed – as you know, we weren't expecting you.

Fola   I've never actually seen you make a bed.

She exits with her luggage. **Rita** *looks at* **Kayode**.

Rita   What are you doing?

Kayode   What?

Rita   Don't act brand new, like you don't know what she is up to. Her bloody job is to encourage people to uproot to that god-forsaken place. She is going to go on at you until you say yes.

Kayode   I didn't say I want to go and live there.

Rita   She is like a shark, she only needs a drop of blood before she . . .

Kayode   I need a break.

Rita   Honey, listen to me. We could both do with a break. Why not Barbados or Dubai?

Kayode   I want to go to Nigeria. I would like to see my mother. She is not getting any younger . . .

Rita   Fly her out here. I will go away and you two can . . .

Kayode   It would be great if you could come too.

Rita   No way. If I come your mother will spend all her time telling me over and over again how I put a curse on you. I don't wanna have to deal with her black-magic mumbo jumbo.

Kayode   She says that as a joke. (*Pause.*) I am not going to force you to come, I'd like you to *want* to come.

Rita   I can't.

Kayode   I need to get away from here, Rita.

Rita   Then go.

Kayode   Sure?

Rita   Can I convince you to stay?

Kayode   I'd only be gone a few weeks, clear my mind a bit. It could help with us.

Silence.

Rita   You can come back into the room now.

Fola (*offstage*)   How do you know I want to come into the room?

She re-enters the room.

So it's settled then. You are going back to Nigeria. I am going to set up a meeting with . . .

Kayode   Slow down, Fola. I am only going for a holiday.

Scene Two

Nigeria. The living room has been transformed into a modern-day living room in Nigeria – spacious and beautifully decorated: marble flooring, an air-conditioning system, leather sofa, with authentic African paintings on the wall. A huge plasma-screen television and an even bigger sound system is in a corner. A glass dining table for six is on the other side. There are bottled soft drinks, Guinness and Star beer on the centre table, with a bowl of ice and some fancy glasses, a bowl of peanuts and two side dishes of plantain chips and puff-puff.

Kunle *is sitting on the sofa with his legs up watching a music channel. A* **Driver** *enters the house carrying two big suitcases followed by* **Kayode** *dressed in a suit.* **Kunle** *jumps off the sofa to shake his hand.*

Kunle   Good evening. We have been expecting you . . . ?

Kayode   Oh hello, and you are –

Kunle   Kunle. Take a seat. Mama will be here shortly. She went to the beauty salon. You know women now, she gone to get the full works, manicure, pedicure – and hair, of course. Mama makes me laugh. She loves spending hours in the hair salon getting her hair all done up only to cover it with a headscarf when it's finished. I don't see the point but . . .

Kayode *looks around the house, taking in the new setting.*

Kayode   Excuse me, but who are you?

Kunle   I am Kunle. Mama has been delayed and asked me to welcome and receive you.

He picks up a bottle. **Kayode** *signals for* **Kunle** *to put it down. He ignores him and pours* **Kayode** *a drink.*

Kunle   We are happy to see you . . . and Mama will be pleased you have arrived safely. Since the news of your visit, she has not stopped talking about you. The way Mama has been acting you would think the King of England himself was arriving in Ijebu-Ode.

Kunle *holds out the drink for* **Kayode**. *He accepts it but does not take a sip, and puts the glass back on the table.* **Kunle** *looks at* **Kayode**, *grinning.*

Kayode   Are you all right there?

Kunle *continues to stare.*

Kunle   Sorry. It is very strange seeing you in the flesh. I feel like I know you personally.

Kayode   Shame I have heard very little about you.

Kunle   So is all of it true?

Kayode   All of what?

Kunle   What I have read about you, and what Mama says also?

Kayode   Depends what you have heard and read.

Kunle   Talking like a true politician.

Kayode   And how does a politician talk, young man?

Kunle   Avoiding the question.

Kayode   Is that what they teach you at school?

Kunle   Taught sir. Not teach. I finished my schooling . . .

Kayode   Is that so?

Mama *enters dressed in an all-white 'iro at buba' (wrapper and top).* **Kayode** *jumps out of his seat as soon as he sees his mother.* **Kunle** *prostrates for* **Mama**, *but she does not notice him.* **Kunle** *gets up.*

Mama   I cannot believe it. Alluhamdululia Rabilliah Al-Amin.

She is in a very good mood. **Kunle** *watches, smiling too. She opens up her arms for a big hug.*

Kayode   Mum.

He gives his mother a hug. She holds him out and takes a look at him, then hugs him again.

Mama   I cannot believe it. Oluwasheun Kayode Rafiq Darmilola Adebukola Adetunji, is that you I am seeing?

Kayode *nods.*

Mama   I said is that you I am seeing? God you are wonderful.

She starts to sing.

Mama   Subhalliah Wallihandulliah Alllllaaah Alllaaah Akbar. [*Thank you God. God is great.*] Thank you God for bringing my son back to me safely. I didn't think I would see this day. The day my son, my only son will finally return home. Adura mi ti gba. [*My prayers have come true.*]

Kayode   I have missed you, Mummy.

Mama (*in Yoruba*)   Ma puro. [*Don't lie.*]

Kayode   I have.

Mama   Is this you I am seeing in the flesh? Please, son, tell me because I am an old woman, tell me that my eyes are not deceiving me.

She hugs him again.

You have finally returned to me. We have missed you.

Kayode   We?

Mama   Yes, we . . . me and your country. We have missed you.

Kunle   Mama, is there anything you want me to do for you?

Mama   Ah, Kunle. Sorry, my boy, I didn't see you there. Have you met my son?

Kunle   Yes, Mama.

Mama *grins at* **Kayode**.

Mama   Kayode have you met Kunle?

Kayode   Yes, Mama.

Mama   My two boys have finally met.

Pause.

Kunle is a wonderful, brilliant, fantastic boy.

Kunle   Oh Mama, please.

Mama   It's true – you know me, I won't say it if it's not true.

Kunle   I wish I can take all the credit but that lies with you. Would you like me to do anything else for you?

Mama   God has given me everything I asked for.

Kunle   I will see you later. (*To* **Kayode**.) Nice to meet you, Brother Kayode.

Kayode   Likewise.

Mama   Will you not be joining us for dinner?

Kunle   I have a meeting with Chief Olowolaye.

Mama *kisses her teeth.* **Kunle** *laughs it off.*

Kunle   I will be sure to pass on your kind regards and greetings.

Mama   You will do no such thing.

Kunle   I will see you later.

Mama   Kunle, wait.

She rummages through her bag and hands him a bag with a bar of soap in it. He opens the bag.

Kunle   Mama, what is all of this now?

Mama   It is for your protection. You have to bath with that soap every morning, and when you bath you make sure you pray and you thank God for everything, and tell him what you want.

Kunle   Yes, Ma.

He prostrates himself to **Mama** *and exits.*

Kayode   I see you haven't stopped taking in strays. You have to be careful, Mummy . . .

Mama   Kunle is no stray. I brought him up to –

Kayode   Where is his family?

Mama   Koni Mama Koni baba. [*He has no mother or father.*] I'm his family now.

She heads over to a table, takes out a photo album and hands it to **Kayode**.

Kayode   Here we go again . . .

Mama   When I tell you that Kunle is special . . . I mean special, special. He appreciates all the help I have given him. He is running in the next elections for local government and, Kayode, oh this town with Kunle at the forefront . . . I am telling you this now, he is going to put it on the map. It's the younger generation that is going to change this country.

Kayode   He looks young – a bit *too* young.

Mama   Don't let that fool you, he is exceptionally brilliant. He cares about Ijebu-Ode and the people of this town. I am very proud of him. In just a few years he has done some amazing things already.

Kayode   With your money, no doubt.

Mama   You see, you see this is why I didn't want to tell you about him. I wanted you to meet him yourself.

Kayode   Like you wanted me to meet Femi, Chuka, Shola, Tunde . . .

Mama   Kunle is not like that at all, at all. Do you know, he lobbied and fought for the children to have free school meals.

She picks up a newspaper article and shows **Kayode**, *as well as a framed picture of her and* **Kunle**.

Mama   A fantastic achievement! More children in this area go to school . . . oh, it's exciting. A brain that remains untrained is a drain on society and I have made sure that Kunle has received the best education possible, like you. Once a former area boy –

Kayode   Your favourite tale of rags to riches . . .

Mama   What Kunle is doing . . . people are starting to understand that education is a right, not a privilege. The class of '66's destructive legacy will be a thing of the past. Oh, Kayode, nobody in this town thought it possible. There were more doubters, but come and see all the people, all of them, that not too many years ago wanted to stone poor Kunle for stealing a loaf of bread, now the same doubters line the street chanting his name. Mark my words, he is going to be the President of Nigeria one of these days.

Kayode   Some things haven't changed.

Mama   We were once . . .

Kayode   Giants of Africa.

Mama   Now we are the laughing stock of the whole world. Kunle gives me great hope. So, are you going to tell your mother what happened to you in London?

Kayode   I've told you already. I just hope that Kunle is not hassling you for money.

Mama   Money keh. Your mother is no pushover. Instead of doubting him you should be thanking him.

Kayode   For what?

Mama   For saving me from dying with a broken heart because my only son refuses to give me a grandchild. Kunle has promised to give me many grandchildren. He also promised he will not run away to London like you.

Kayode   The way you talk is like I abandoned you.

Mama   Is it not because I carry my body to come to the blasted country of yours that you see me?

Kayode Why do you hate London so much?

Mama Because the weather over there hates me. It's always trying to attack me.

Kayode The way you talk is like the weather is a person.

Mama It is a person o . . . English weather is a soul-stealer.

Kayode Stop exaggerating now.

Silence.

Mama I am glad you are divorcing that useless wife of yours o.

Kayode I am not divorcing Rita.

Mama A mother can wish.

Kayode That is not very nice Mummy. She didn't come here cos she thinks you hate her.

Mama I do hate her. I still don't understand how that barren witch managed to get you to marry her.

Kayode I married her cos I love her. We choose not to have children, Mother.

Mama The Alufa has told me it is not love.

Kayode You still go and see a witch doctor.

Mama He is a man of God.

Kayode Whatever, they are a waste of money.

Silence.

Mama Kayode, do you pray?

Kayode What has that got to do with anything?

Mama Answer the question.

Kayode No.

Mama Do not let God hear you say that o. The Alufa told me to pray for you and I pray for you – it is my prayers that keep you safe. I pray for you every day. I have been praying since the day you left for you to find your way back home. The Alufa told me God said to him he sent you on a pilgrimage to find yourself, and once you have completed that journey you will find your way back home, and that's the reason you failed in that miserable country.

Kayode   I am here to rest, Mummy.

Mama   I want you to do something for me, Kayode. I am not asking you for anything big.

Kayode   What is it?

Mama   I want you to teach Kunle everything you know. He lacks one thing . . . great council. He has many people falling over themselves backing his campaign to satisfy their own selfish needs. This Chief Olowolaye has dug his claws deep into Kunle. He is trying to poison my boy against me. Help me help him.

She gets up and hugs him.

Mama   My boy, look at you, tell me I am dreaming.

She jumps around and begins singing the popular closing Islamic prayer, Fatia.

Mama   Bismillah Hir Rahmaanir Raheem.

Kayode   Be careful – don't want to break a hip.

Mama   Alhamdo Lillahi Rabbil Aalameen. Ar Rahmaanir Raheem. Maaliki Yaomid Deen iyya Kana Budoo Wa iyya kanastaeen ihdinas Siratual Mustaqeem Siratual Lazeena An Amtaa Alaihim Ghairil Maghdoobe Alaihim Walad Dualleen.

Mama *and* **Kayode**   Ameen.

She wipes his face, crosses her arms over his chest.

Mama   That is the only bit you know. Come on, do your Michael 'Jacksin'.

Kayode   Oh no, Mum. I can't . . .

Mama   Just this once, for me.

Kayode   I am old now.

Mama   Are you going to break an old woman's heart?

Kayode   Emotional blackmail, Mummy. Are you really
going to . . .

She claps her hands and starts singing.

Mama   'You know I'm bad, I'm bad you know it . . .'

Kayode *gets up and does the moonwalk and a 'Michael Jackson dance
move-he-he and all'.* **Mama** *hugs him.*

Mama   Oh my son, welcome home.

Scene Three

Nigeria. A few days have passed. **Kayode**, **Kunle** *and* **Mama** *are
in the living room.* **Kayode** *and* **Kunle** *are both eating some egusi
and pounded yam.* **Kayode** *is using a fork while* **Kunle** *is using his
hands. The two men discuss their thoughts on politics as* **Mama** *cuts
them meat.*

Kunle   Brother Kayode, let me finish now, ah ah. *I am not
saying that fraud and corruption is* not *a problem.* What I am saying
is our *biggest problem* – what keeps this country oppressed – is
our need to look to the outsider to tell us how to act, what
type of Nigerians we should be. We are constantly seeking
approval from others . . .

Kayode   Who are the others?

Kunle (*in Yoruba*)   Eh ma binu sa – [*don't be mad*] but it's
people like you. You come here with your *white* views and your
white way of working and try to embed them into our society.

Kayode   I'm not white!

Kunle   All you foreigners think and act like a white 'persin'.
What you fail to realise is that this is not the white man's land.

Kayode *looks over at* **Mama***, who is shaking her head agreeing with* **Kunle***.*

Kunle   I am sick to death of 'black crusaders' who have taken the place of the white ones who come here and tell us how we should act. This is Africa, and we have our own way of doing things. The day we stop worrying about what others think about us –

Kayode   And what are you?

Kunle   Hustlers. I know, Mama, you don't like the word . . .

Mama   You had me at Kayode being white –

Kayode   Pardon . . .

Mama   But lost me at 'hustler'.

Kayode   Are you two colour-blind?

They both ignore him.

Kunle   I am a hustler till the day that I die, mehn, and so is every Nigerian.

Kayode   I am a Nigerian and I am not a hustler.

Kunle   You are an Englishman. You live an easy life. You don't have to hustle.

Kayode   Who told you that?

Kunle   Mama kept me informed. Is it not why you didn't come back to visit her?

Mama (*to* **Kayode**)   He's right.

Kunle (*to* **Kayode**)   A hustler to me is someone that grinds, works from morning to night to make ends meet.

Kayode   Then in that case I have a right to be a called a hustler.

Kunle   'English' hustler.

He bursts into laughter, as does **Mama***.*

Kunle   It's a very different thing.

Kayode (*to* **Kunle**)   We shall have to agree to disagree.

Kunle   I agree we need to disagree!

Mama (*to* **Kayode**)   You? A hustler? (*To* **Kunle**.) When he was a young boy like this, Kayode was too scared to go to the market by himself – people were always taking his money from him.

Kayode   No need to tell tales now, Mother.

Mama (*to* **Kunle**)   As a child, Kayode was very weak. There was this girl . . . She would always make Kayode cry . . .

Kayode   Ramatu was not a girl, she was a beast.

Mama   She was smaller than you . . .

Kayode   Can you drop it, Mother!

Mama   Pele, my hustling son.

He gives her an evil look as she smirks.

Mama   I agree with you, Kayode, the main problem is greed and corruption. Nothing more, nothing less.

Kayode (*to* **Kunle**)   Mama has settled the argument. Corruption *is* Nigeria's biggest problem!

Mama   Hold on a second, Kayode, it is a worldwide problem.

Kunle   Do not forget we have our eyes on the world too. In your country we know a *rich* man can buy a super-injunction and keep his affairs quiet. That is corruption, isn't it, Mama?

Mama (*to* **Kunle**)   Yes, but in England it is not respected, it will be exposed, and you will be disgraced. When has there ever been a disgraced minister in this country?

Kayode   EXACTLY!

Mama   What weighs heavily on my heart is that there is enough money to make Nigeria better for everyone. There is too much mismanagement of funds. The people at the bottom

all aspire to be rich, the people at the top flaunt their wealth.
Look at that Chief Olowolaye – uneducated buffoon. (*To*
Kunle.) How many houses does he have in England,
America? He has money in banks in Switzerland, Dubai, you
name it. (*To* **Kayode**.) His politics is do or die.

Kunle   When are you going to stop your conspiracy theories
about the Chief?

Mama   What happened to Dr Kareem?

She pours out drinks for **Kunle** *and* **Kayode**.

Kunle   An unfortunate car crash.

Mama   Exactly.

Kunle   Can we have a conversation without bringing up the
Chief's name?

Mama   Then don't allow him to brainwash you.

Kunle (*to* **Kayode**)   Everywhere you go in the world –

Kayode   And where in the world have you been?

Kunle   Chief Olowo . . .

Mama   I thought we were not allowed to say his name!

Kunle *gives* **Mama** *an evil stare.*

Kunle   You never let me talk.

Mama   Talk!

Kayode *and* **Kunle** *both eat their meals in silence. Both enjoy the
pieces of meat picked up on their plates.* **Kunle** *shakes his head.*

Kunle *watches* **Kayode** *as he uses the fork to eat his pounded yam.*

Kayode   What?

Kunle   Why do you eat like a white persin?

Mama *laughs.*

Kayode   I'm being polite.

Kunle   Going against our culture is not being polite. It is saying that you don't think our culture is any good.

Kayode   I'm eating like me. (*To* **Mama**.) Haven't I always eaten like this? Tell him. This is the way I've always eaten.

Kunle   We eat with our hands because we like to feel the texture of the different foods we consume. *We need to stop apologising to the world about who we are!* We are unashamedly Nigerian from the way we talk to the way we eat.

Kayode   Where do you learn these things?

Mama   It's the Chief, he who must not be named.

Kunle   Mama!

Mama   Your Chief Olowolaye is a low-down dirty scoundrel.

Kayode   Low-down dirty scoundrel?

Mama   Yes. That is what he is.

Kunle *and* **Kayode** *laugh.*

Mama   What . . .

Kayode   I forgot you do that.

Mama   Kini? [*What?*]

Kayode   Take references from films.

Mama   I didn't get it from a film.

Kayode   Mother!

Kunle   It was on the TV yesterday. *Dirty Rotten Scoundrels*?

Mama   I don't remember. I am going to bed jor.

She gets up to head to bed.

Odaro.

Kunle *gets up.* **Mama** *gestures for him to sit down.*

Mama   Finish your conversation.

She winks and smiles at **Kayode**. *She goes to leave.*

Mama (*to* **Kayode**)   Will you be joining me at Asalatu
tomorrow?

Kayode   Erm . . .

Mama   I will like to see you come to the mosque at least
once during your stay. Sho gbo? [*Do you understand?*]

Kayode   Yes, Ma.

Mama   Both of you better finish your food.

Kayode *and* **Kunle**   Yes, Mummy . . .

Kunle   I mean Mama.

She exits.

Kayode *looks at* **Kunle**.

Kunle   I'm sorry, Brother Kayode.

Kayode   No need to –

Kunle   Hearing you call her 'Mummy' has probably just –

Kayode   It's fine.

*They both eat their food in awkward silence, trying to avoid taking pieces
of the pounded yam at the same time.*

Kayode   My mum told me you used to be a former gang
member?

Kunle   'Gang', keh? Not at all.

Kayode   An area boy?

Kunle   Out of necessity.

Silence.

I wouldn't be where I am today without Mama's help and
guidance. I owe her my life. Part of why I am getting involved
in politics is because I know how happy it will make her. I just
want to make Mama happy. She has never asked me for

anything but to promise one small thing. To give her grandchildren.

Kayode   Technically you can't give her grandchildren – you're not related to her.

Kunle   And you wonder why we look at you like a white man?

Kayode   Excuse me.

Kunle   Sorry, Brother Kayode. Awon Yoruba ni wa now. [*We are Yoruba people.*] You don't have to share blood to share family. Mama ni ni kan ni. [*Mama has been the only mother I know.*]

Pause.

She has brought me up as her son . . . Not to say I am taking your place . . . your junior brother.

Scene Four

Nigeria. **Kayode** *and* **Kunle** *are in a bar.*

Barman   Mr English, sa can I give you some advice?

Kayode   That is not my name.

Barman   Sa. If you keep giving your money away to every beggar that comes in here, they will keep coming back o. They already know you are a tourist to this –

Kayode   Omo Ijebu-Ode ni me. [*I am a child of this town.*] And I know how to handle myself well well.

Barman   Sorry, sa.

He walks off.

Kayode   All of this Mr English, tourist stuff is starting to rub me up the wrong way.

Kunle   Just ignore them.

Kayode   I know what this place is like, I just . . . . I just remember it a bit differently. I can't . . . There are people out there willing to work. Graft, clean toilets for less than ten pounds . . . educated people, and they are reduced to begging day in day out for a bite to eat. (*To* **Barman**.) I'm not shocked by it I'm just . . .

Barman *puts down the drinks.*

Kunle   Anyone with enough money to educate themselves finds a way out of this country.

Kayode (*to* **Kunle**)   I keep hearing this country is on the up. My friend Fola is back in London right now, enticing British Nigerians to return to the promised land.

Barman   Promised land? This is a lawless country, no electricity, poor roads, bad hospitals . . . Only the rich enjoy life in Nigeria. The poor suffer o. But it is not your problem, sa . . . don't feel guilty for it. You are not the government.

Barman *exits.*

Kayode   You have been a great tour guide.

Kunle   It's not a problem, Brother Kayode.

Kayode   I hope Rita will like all this stuff. She can be very picky sometimes.

Kunle   Why didn't she come with you?

Kayode   She is not a fan of Nigeria, and my mother is not a fan of hers.

Kunle   I got the impression from Mama she would rather you married a black woman.

Kayode   My wife is black.

Kunle   Oh, Mama said your wife was oyinbo.

Kayode   Sometimes my mother talks out of her . . .

Chief Olowolaye *makes a big entrance. He is dressed in a big 'agbada'.*

Chief Olowolaye   Kunle Kunz, my boy.

Kunle *prostrates for* **Chief Olowolaye**, *who gestures for* **Kunle** *to get up and give him a hug.*

Kunle   Afternoon, sa!

Chief Olowolaye   Drinks for everybody! Today is a gooood day! Thanking you, please.

Kunle   Chief, I'd like you to meet . . .

Chief Olowolaye   Kayode Adetunji MP of London. I follow you on Twitter. You are welcome.

Kayode   I've deactivated my account!

Chief Olowolaye   Don't have to be on there for people to stop talking. You have ruffled many feathers in your country. Anyway, sha, their loss is our gain. We are happy to receive you.

He lifts up his hand to shake **Kayode**'s *hand.* **Kayode** *shakes his hand.*

Kunle   Brother Kayode, this is Chief . . .

Chief Olowolaye   Olowolaye. What are you drinking?

Kayode *raises his glass.*

Chief Olowolaye   You are drinking a poor man's drink.

He stands up to address the whole bar.

CHAMPAGNE FOR EVERYBODY! And for my friend the MP Ace of Spades only. Barman, make you bring a crate for my new friend.

The **Barman** *slowly walks over and tries to whisper to* **Chief Olowolaye**.

Barman   Chief, sa, we don't have Ace of −

The **Chief** *grabs the* **Barman**.

Chief Olowolaye   What are you telling me?

Barman   We don't have any . . .

Kayode *gets up and helps the* **Barman**.

Kayode   I don't need a drink.

The **Barman** *prostrates himself for the* **Chief**.

Barman   I'm sorry, sa.

Kayode   Young man, get up.

Chief Olowolaye   Yes, get up and go and get your manager.

Barman   My manager is not –

Kayode   You don't need to get your manager.

Chief Olowolaye   MP of London, you are right. (*To* **Barman**.) I will deal with you later, just bring me any drink. But for now – (*To* **Kayode**.) Let's get down to business.

Kayode *looks at* **Kunle** *as* **Chief Olowolaye** *places a wad of cash on the table.*

Kayode   What business?

Chief Olowolaye (*to* **Kunle**)   I like him! (*To* **Kayode**.) We are in a bar drinking and socialising. I stand corrected. Today's business is also our pleasure. Let's get down to pleasure. So Kayode MP of London. It is a big pleasure to meet you. We are honoured to have you as part of our campaign.

Kayode   Excuse me?

Chief Olowolaye   Let us cut all the *'shitbull'*. You are here to invest in our campaign. Your political career in England has ended and you are back home to –

Kayode   Not at all . . .

Chief Olowolaye   Kunle told me that you would one hundred per cent guaranteed be joining our campaign.

Kayode   Really . . .

Kunle   No no, sa! I didn't say that.

Chief Olowolaye   Are you not interested in what we do here?

Kunle   Brother Kayode is just here to –

Chief Olowolaye   Oh forgive me, where are my manners?

He opens a bag and hands **Kayode** *a watch.*

Chief Olowolaye   We thank you in advance for your generosity.

He winks at **Kayode**. **Kayode** *does not take the watch.*

Chief Olowolaye   Give to receive, abi.

Kunle   Chief, Brother Kayode isn't going to be –

Kayode (*to* **Kunle**)   Can you explain what is going on here please?

Kunle   What the Chief is trying to say –

Chief Olowolaye   Kunle, at this moment in time myself I am very confused.

Kunle   I am sorry, Chief. I probably didn't make it clear enough why I thought you should meet Brother Kayode . . .

Chief Olowolaye   So he can contribute to our campaign –

Kunle   Because you wanted to hear first hand the advice he has been giving me . . .

Kayode   Would have been nice to know a meeting was being set up.

Kunle   It's not a meeting.

Chief Olowolaye   My time is very precious . . .

Kunle   I know and . . . I thought . . .

Chief Olowolaye *gets up.*

Kunle   Chief, wait.

Chief Olowolaye   Due to the fact that you are not here to discuss possible investment . . . as you can see I am a very busy man . . .

Kunle   Chief, please, I think that −

Chief Olowolaye   I have told you before these people from London are not serious. You need to stop bringing these cowards to come and meet me. They don't care about this country, that is why they run away overseas in the first place. Whilst good people like us stay on here to deal with our problems head on.

Kayode   Hold up a second. I never asked or knew I was here to meet or discuss anything.

Chief Olowolaye   When people were protesting, marching on the street over fuel subsidies, were you here? NO. You were back in England, in Mayfair sitting on your throne.

Kayode   I live in Croydon.

Chief Olowolaye   You English and Yankees love to sit in your castles and complain about this land but never want to get your hands dirty.

Kayode *laughs.*

Chief Olowolaye   I am glad you find me funny.

Kayode   Have you been to London?

Chief Olowolaye   Of course. I have two apartments in Primrose Hill.

Kayode (*sarcastically*)   Naturally.

Chief Olowolaye   Why are you here?

Kayode   To enjoy a quiet drink . . .

Chief Olowolaye   My question pertains to Nigeria.

Kayode   I am here to relax and −

Chief Olowolaye   Awon Oyinbo e. [*These white people.*]

Kayode   I'M NIGERIAN!

Chief Olowolaye (*begins to laugh loudly*)   You are only a Nigerian by name. Put 230,000 on the table now.

Kayode   What for?

Chief Olowolaye   Can you put the money on the table or not?

Kayode (*to* **Kunle**)   Is this guy serious?

Kunle   Chief is trying to –

Chief Olowolaye   In view of the fact that your friend cannot produce – how much is it in pounds, roughly £1,000 – without questioning or being informed about the purposes, I suggest you take yourself back to your country.

Kayode   Is this who you are running a campaign with?

Chief Olowolaye   The whole town knows your mother is losing her mind. I see the banana doesn't fall far from the tree.

Kayode   Who the hell do you think you are?

Chief Olowolaye   Is it me you are talking to like that?

Kunle (*to* **Chief Olowolaye**)   Please, sa. I'm sorry.

Kayode (*to* **Kunle**)   Don't apologise for this mutton dressed as lamb.

Chief Olowolaye   Are you calling me an animal?

Kayode   Yes.

Kunle   Brother Kayode, you can't say things like that.

Kayode   This man is clearly uneducated . . .

Chief Olowolaye   You, this simpleton, bastard of a child. Who are you calling uneducated?

Kayode   YOU!

Kunle *begins to prostrate himself.*

Kayode   Kunle, get up now.

Chief Olowolaye   I have told you, Kunle, this useless family will be your downfall.

Kayode   Shut up! Get up, Kunle!

Chief Olowolaye   I am the one you are telling to shut up?

Kayode   Yes. Full of hot air . . .

The **Chief** *begins to remove his 'agbada' as* **Kunle** *and the* **Barman** *try to hold him back.*

Chief Olowolaye   I am going to beat this boy senseless today.

Kunle   Wait, sa. This is all . . . Let's discuss this like men.

Chief Olowolaye *leaps and tries to grab* **Kayode**, *who stands still and only backs away slightly.* **Chief Olowolaye** *pushes* **Kunle** *and the* **Barman** *but they continue to beg him.*

Chief Olowolaye   I am CHIEF OLOWOLAYE and I DEMAND RESPECT. Do I look like your age-mate?

Kunle *prostrates himself in front of the* **Chief** *again.*

Kayode   Get up, Kunle.

Chief Olowolaye   ARE YOU PEOPLE SEEING THIS?!

Kunle   Chief please . . . (*To* **Kayode**.) Please apologise to the Chief . . .

Kayode   I am waiting for *his* apology.

Chief Olowolaye   I demand in this very instant moment that you ask for forgiveness for your defiance of my authority.

Kayode   Kunle, let's go.

Kayode *starts to gather his bags.*

Kunle   Brother Kayode, you can't go until you –

Chief Olowolaye   I am waiting.

Kayode   Keep waiting.

Kunle   Chief please Mo gbe e. [*I am begging you.*] Ejo sa
[*Please sir.*]

Chief Olowolaye   DO YOU PEOPLE SEE THIS! These
people from London need to understand they can't come here
and throw their weight! You are all witnesses to this
abomination! I AM CHIEF OLOWOLAYE.

Kayode (*to* **Kunle**)   Are you coming?

Chief Olowolaye (*to* **Kunle**)   In the present situation, if
you walk out that door with that man . . .

Kayode   Kunle –

Kunle   Please, Chief . . . Brother Kayode, let's sit down and
talk like men.

Kayode *storms out.* **Kunle** *looks towards the door and then back at
the* **Chief***. He stays.*

Scene Five

Nigeria. **Kayode** *is in the living room pacing up and down while*
Mama *is sitting in the chair.*

Kayode   Why are you not upstairs packing his stuff?

Mama   Joko. [*Sit down.*]

Kayode   That man insulted you and Kunle didn't say a
word.

Mama   This is why you need to help . . .

Kayode   If you're not going to pack his stuff, I will.

Mama   No. Kunle is my boy and . . .

Kayode   I am your boy!

Pause.

Mother, stop feeling guilty about your wealth. Stop wasting it on these street rats.

Voice (*offstage*)   Wait, sa! Please, sa, you cannot go in there! Mama, Mama!

Police Commissioner *Samson Ali-Amin enters.* **Mama** *immediately bends down and greets him.*

Mama   Police Commissioner, sa . . .

Police Commissioner   Is this your son?

Mama   Please come and sit down.

Police Commissioner   Kayode Adetunji, follow me down to the station now . . .

Mama   Would you like a drink?

Police Commissioner   I'm here on official business.

Kayode   It's a good thing you're here. (*To* **Mama**.) The Chief . . .

Police Commissioner (*to* **Kayode**)   Follow me down to the station. NOW! This is a very serious matter. A crime has been committed.

Kayode   Right!

Mama   Kayode, ma soro. [*Kayode, don't talk.*] Police Commissioner, there has been a misunderstanding. You know me.

Police Commissioner   It is out of respect for you that I have not sent my officer down to arrest your son.

Kayode   WHAT? Arrest? For what?

Police Commissioner   You're being charged for physical serious assault on Chief Olowolaye!

Kayode (*to* **Mama**)   Is this a joke?

Mama   Ah-ah. I am sure Police Commissioner Mr Samson Ali-Amin wants to get this sorted as quickly as possible.

Kayode (*to* **Police Commissioner**)   How much did he pay you?

Police Commissioner   Excuse me?

Mama   Kayode kilo she eh now? [*What is wrong with you?*]

Kayode   Answer the question?

Police Commissioner (*to* **Mama**)   Talk to your son?

Mama (*to* **Kayode**)   Kayode, let's not make this worse than what it is. You go and apologise to the Chief and . . .

Kayode   I am not going anywhere.

Mama   Kayode, we have to listen to him.

Police Commissioner   I am not going to wait any more. If you do not come peacefully, I will have no choice but to take you by force.

Kayode *sits.*

Mama   Kayode, what are you doing?

Scene Six

England. Back in London **Fola** *and* **Rita** *are in the living room surrounded by boxes. On one side is a box of chocolates and on the other a shipment of handbags.*

Rita *is opening the boxes, going through an inventory.*

Fola   What am I going to do with all this Snickers now?

Rita   I don't usually take much pleasure in telling you I told you so, but in this case because I did tell you so over a hundred times, I take a lot of pleasure in telling you I told you so.

Fola   This is all your fault! Why do you have such a small freezer?

Rita   I didn't know people store chocolate in freezers.

Fola   You are Nigerian.

Rita   So by default I have to have a bush mentality?

Fola   'Sarcasam' doesn't suit you.

Rita   It's sarcasm?

Fola   As a Nigerian, your house should be well equipped. Where is your standing freezer?

Rita   We don't need one.

Fola   I hate to correct you . . . you do. There is a lot of things your house is lacking . . . For instance where is your egbalewa? [*broom.*]

Rita   We have a Hoover.

Fola   You see . . . basic common essentials you don't have.

Rita   Okay, Fola. You're right, I'm wrong. Happy?

Fola   In the bathroom you have no bucket.

Rita   Don't even go there. I've never had a bucket bath, and there is no way you're telling me you still bathe with a bowl and bucket.

Fola   I like to keep it old school!

Rita   Lying to prove a pointless point . . .

Fola   Don't get your knickers twisted.

Silence.

Rita   When did you say you were flying back?

Fola   I didn't. Tomorrow early early morning I have a very important meeting with – you remember Fumilaye? I have convinced her to come and work for Central Bank of Nigeria. Human Resources Director.

Rita   How do you even plan on getting this through customs?

Fola   I have my ways.

Rita Won't it melt?

Fola That's why you should have a freezer!

Rita As much as you say you hate this country, deep down you know you can't live without it or its resources.

Fola Don't get me started on resources. If these people did not come to Africa . . .

Rita Ahhh, does everything have to be a deba –

Fola You – this woman you have changed to. You used to be the one drummed all of these things into my head, and now the simple mention of the word Nigeria or Africa – your nose is up in the air like you have smelt something dirty.

Rita I am tired of the moaning. If they did a survey to find out what race moans the most I can guarantee it that black people will be at the top of the list, and at the top of the black list Nigerians.

Fola What you call moaning we call expressing ourselves – Madam Hinglish.

Rita English.

Fola Listen here . . .

Rita Listen –

Fola No no no. You list'ten –

Rita It's listen –

Fola Oh-o. You are now the pronunciation police?

Rita Yes, if you're the furniture police.

Fola Why is everything a competition for you? Better start being nice to me . . . When I get a husband and a family you will not see me in this place o. So you better use the time you have with me wisely and stop picking on me.

Rita And when are you going to get a husband?

Fola I am waiting for the right man to find me.

Rita   You are not getting any younger.

Fola   Says the woman who has been married for how long and has not yet had her first child. Why don't you just tell everybody what the problem is. There is so many different treatments out there that can help you . . .

Rita   I don't have a problem having children.

Fola   Then why don't you have one? Bite my head off for saying this, but you can be very selfish sometimes, Rita.

Rita *is hurt by the comment but remains silent.*

Fola   The second I get married, I will be pregnant within six month mark my words o. There is no point in making money, making money and just spending it on yourself. After a while the loneliness sinks in. I'm sure Kayode would love to have a little boy running around the house. Only God knows how you managed to keep a man for so long.

Rita   I'll tell you how, it's because I know how to drop it like it's hot.

She shakes her bum.

Fola   If you wanna keep your man's attention you have to learn some better moves than that.

Rita *leaves.*

Scene Seven

Nigeria. A battered and bruised **Kayode** *arrives home, followed by* **Mama***. He sits in the chair rubbing his bruised face.*

Long silence.

Mama   Are you hungry?

Silence.

She stares at **Kayode***, who is clearly in a lot of pain.*

Awkward silence.

Mama   I still think we should go to the hospital.

Kayode *ignores* **Mama***.*

Mama   Just for a check-up.

Silence.

Kayode . . .

Kayode   2.5 million.

Silence.

(*To himself.*)   2.5 million.

Pause.

4,500 pounds.

Mama   What did you want me to do?

Silence.

Kayode (*to himself*)   2.5 million.

Mama *gets on her knees and tries to hold* **Kayode***'s hands. He shrugs her off.*

Mama   What did you want me to do, Kayode?

Kayode   NOTH . . . (*Screams in pain.*) . . . AHHHHH . . . NOTHING! You just needed to do nothing.

Mama *drops to the floor.*

Mama   Jor omo mi. [*Please, my son.*] Please don't be mad with me.

Kayode   Stop begging.

He pushes her off.

Paying that bribe –

Mama   It was not a bribe.

Kayode *talks through the pain.*

Kayode   – makes you one of them.

Mama   Look at your face – don't fool yourself, they could have done worse.

Kayode   AND YOU SHOULD HAVE LET THEM! (*In pain.*) AHHHHH.

Mama   This is not England, you could have been killed . . .

Kayode   I KNOW THIS ISN'T FUCKING ENGLAND.

Mama   Ma binu Omo mi. [*Don't be mad, my child.*] Maybe you should go back to London. I will come with you . . .

Kayode   No.

Mama   I am telling you, you will be safer back home . . .

Kayode   NO!

She tries to go and hug him. He pushes her off.

Kunle *enters the living room.*

Mama   Where have you been? Do you know what Olowolaye has put Kayode through?

Kunle *prostrates himself on the floor.*

Kunle   Brother Kayode, I tried to . . .

Mama (*to* **Kunle**)   Omo mi. [*My child.*] Please talk to your senior brother.

Kunle   Yes, Ma. I didn't know he was going to get you arrested. I stayed to calm him down, but you humiliated him . . . Do not poke a sleeping lion.

Kayode   Oh, trust me, the lion has already been poked.

Kunle   The Chief is a powerful man. He has friends in high places.

Mama (*to* **Kayode**)   And you were lucky today, he didn't do his worst. What will you be proving if you carry this on, eh?

Kayode (*to* **Kunle**)   Do you owe him money?

Kunle   No.

Kayode   Is he blackmailing you?

Kunle   No.

Kayode   What does he have on you?

Kunle   You won't understand.

Kayode   Try explaining.

Kunle   He has been a father to me . . .

Kayode   And my mother?

Mama   As you can see, Kayode, it is better for Kunle to have Olowolaye on his side than as his enemy.

Kayode *turns to leave.*

Kunle   I can help him, Brother Kayode.

Kayode   Who?

Kunle   THE CHIEF! I know what people say about him and what he does, but I know once we start changing this town, the Chief will change his ways. I promise you. Look at me.

He stands in front of **Kayode**.

The Chief is a product of his generation. All crabs in a bucket fighting to be at the top. Once we win the election, once we start changing this town –

Kayode   You tell that Chief of yours he has messed with the wrong man – wrong Englishman.

Scene Eight

England. The living room is full of boxes. **Rita** *and* **Fola** *are both on the floor going through the boxes.* **Rita** *takes out a brand-new designer bag.* **Fola** *places the bag on a stool and starts taking pictures.*

Fola Remind me again why we are not doing this in your boutique?

Rita More space here

Fola Why can't we hire a photographer to do this now, ah ah . . .

Rita You offered to help. I can do it by myself if it's a problem for you.

Fola I am just saying, although I am more skilled than you, these pictures should be left in the hands of a professional photographer.

Rita I'm not wasting my money on a photographer when I can do a good job myself.

Fola Has Kayode called again?

Rita Why is my relationship always at the top of your agenda?

Fola Don't you miss him?

Rita Drop it now Fola!

Silence.

Fola Surely these photos won't be good enough for the website?

Rita Yes, they will.

Fola I didn't really like the design and the site is not very user-friendly if you ask me. It is very basic and boring and ugly and . . .

Rita ENOUGH, FOLA!

Fola What?

Rita Stop taking digs.

Fola You don't want me to talk, I won't talk.

Silence.

When I do have something positive to say, you don't seem to ever want to hear it – that is why you only focus on my corrections.

Rita What have you ever said that is positive?

Fola If I tell you, you will bite my head off!

Rita Just say it.

Fola You sure?

Rita *shoots* **Fola** *a look.*

Fola The best advice I have given you to date is encouraging you to come back home to Nigeria.

Rita (*looking up*) Did you put her on this earth to torture me?

Fola Who are you talking to?

Rita God!

Fola I am your friend, Rita. A friend has to tell a friend where they messed up their lives and how they can improve it. I want what is best for you and Kayode.

Rita For the last time, Fola, keep your Nigerian dream!

Fola It has more prospects than this your European dream you are chasing.

Rita Really, and what is the Nigerian dream?

Fola It cannot be defined at this present moment. Nigeria is yearning for change, I can tell you, and I am not saying this because you are my friend, but you are the change needed. Kayode is there.

Rita On holiday!

Fola   I mean, open your eyes, Rita – your shop is failing.

Rita   My shop is not failing.

Fola   Don't lie to yourself, jare, it is failing. People in this country do not have any money for their pockets. Come and open a shop in Nigeria.

Rita   Stop.

Fola   Omo Nigeria entered into the 2008 so-called great recession with 60 million dollars in reserves. How much is your country in debt? Look at Dubai. I can bet you there are people out there kicking themselves for missing out of the development of Dubai. Nobody thought it was possible for a wasteland desert to become one of the greatest cities in the world. I promise you, Nigeria is next. I am working with my boss to build the biggest mall, shopping mall in Lagos. Bigger than your Westfields. I am offering you the chance to pick out one of the outlets and sell your handbags – make it an international range. Imagine you have a Boutique Lagos. Ijebu . . . Abuja . . .

Rita   You want me to dump my clients for a clientele who are more interested in China fake?

Fola   You are starting to offend me.

Rita   Let's be honest, Fola. You want me to go back so you can keep Kayode close to you . . .

Fola   Ah-ah. Where has this come from?

Rita   I saw how fast you rushed over here.

Fola   If I only came for Kayode, what am I still doing here with you?

Rita   I know what you're playing at, Fola. You know Kay loves me, and where I go he goes . . .

Fola   Are you mad?

Rita   From the day one you have been scheming –

Fola   That's a lie. If after all these years you do not believe
that I am your true friend, then I am wasting my time with
you. If you're insecure about your relationship, don't put it on
me? YOU SHOULD KNOW ME!

Rita   AND YOU SHOULD KNOW ME! For as long as
I've been with Kayode you have been trying to change me.
Trying to make me into this African wife I never wanted to be.
The cooking, the cleaning, the clothes and now your new thing
is to make me pack up my bag and go to live in a place –

Fola   YOU ARE NIGERIAN!

Rita   I'm not!

Fola   Your parents are . . .

Rita   British!

Fola   Don't be foolish, your parents are Nigerian.

Rita   No, my grandparents were and I never met them. So
I'm not Nigerian! My mother and my father were born here
and they have never been to Nigeria in their whole lives. I only
knew about stew from you!

Fola   What happened to the Rita who wanted to trace her
roots and find out about her heritage? The Rita I met in the
library searching for –

Rita   I got tired. This is where I belong.

Fola   And your husband?

Rita   Here with me.

Fola   You have lost the plot? Only white people belong in
this country. Do you think even if a white man was born in
Africa he can call himself African? The colour of your skin
automatically tells the world you are not from this land. Keep
fooling yourself, just know that everyone you meet, everywhere
you go, people will ask you where you are from. Even if they
won't know straight away because of your accent, they will still
ask where your parents are from, and if you tell them British,

next question will always be where are your grandparents from, and will *only* be satisfied till you say Nigeria . . . You never like to hear the truth. Fighting to be accepted in a place you will never be accepted.

Rita   GUESS WHAT FOLA? I'M NOT AS STUPID AS YOU THINK I AM! I will never be accepted over there either. I've been there before, ridiculed for not understanding the language or customs. That place stinks, it's too hot and I don't want to be swatting flies away from my face every minute. I need some air.

Fola   Nigeria is your country.

Rita   No, it's yours.

She exits.

Scene Nine

Nigeria. **Kayode** *is in the living room. He is on his laptop, frantically typing away.*

Mama *and* **Kunle** *enter the room.*

Kayode (*to* **Kunle**)   Kunle I'm glad you're here. I want you both to see this.

He hands them some printouts.

Kunle   'It is not possible to reform internally because those that have risen through the ranks are part of the corrupted system. But with international support we can be sure to reform the police force and restore it to its former glory.'

Kayode   Do you like it?

Kunle   What are you saying, Brother Kayode?

Kayode   That is the bit I like the most. This is where I got things wrong in London. The campaign wasn't about the people, I made them feel like outsiders . . . Rita was right . . .

But here being the outsider works to my advantage. (*To* **Kunle**.) We can be a force to be reckoned with. The outsider and the insider working together.

Kunle *finishes reading the document and is completely shocked.*

Kunle   Let me get this straight, you're running against me?

Kayode   No, with you. This way you part with the Chief without sacrificing your goals.

Kunle (*to* **Kayode**)   I HAVE SWEATED DAY IN AND DAY OUT and you think you can waltz in here and just take it from me with your re-colonisation ideas.

Kayode   Reform, not re-colonisation.

Kunle   You want the British police force to come and train Nigerians.

Kayode   The British police created the Nigerian police . . . It's a step in the right direction. Once we have a safe and stable environment we can start to tackle the problems this country is facing.

Kunle (*to* **Kayode**)   You want to steal my job so you can bring all your friends and give them contracts . . .

Kayode   My brother, you're missing the point . . .

Kunle   You are trying to take my job, you stupid man!

Kayode   Kunle! Don't forget yourself.

Kunle   I don't give a shit, mehn. Why are you doing this? Why? Does my relationship with your mother affect you that much?

Kayode   This has got nothing to do with my mother. This is about Olowolaye.

Kunle   I DON'T WANT TO RUN AGAINST THE CHIEF!

Kayode   The only way you can be sure to get rid of him is if we go against him together.

Mama *continues to read the document.*

Kunle (*to* **Mama**)   Why are you not telling him to stop?

Kayode   This town needs fresh blood.

Kunle   AND THAT IS ME! I AM THE CHANGE THIS TOWN NEEDS. (*To* **Mama**.) Eba omo e soro oh. [*Talk to your child.*]

Mama   Wait. I think Kayode might be on to something.

Silence.

Kunle *shakes his head in disappointment.*

Kunle   Mama, no.

Mama   This is a good proposal. Very good.

Kunle (*to* **Kayode**)   I'm sorry, okay. I'm sorry for what the Chief and the Police Commissioner did to you.

Kayode   It is not about that any more.

Kunle   I said I was sorry. You can forget about this nonsense now. Sorry!

Kayode   Kunle . . .

Kunle   Running against me *is not* a solution or an option.

Mama   Kunle, working with your brother is . . .

Kunle   Brother Kayode will be the first to agree that *we're not brothers*!

Mama   Kilo faye now. [*It hasn't come to that.*]

Kunle (*to* **Kayode**)   Why do you oyinbo people think that you can save us? We are not as stupid as you think or handicapped that we can't help ourselves. Things do not work out for you over there so you think that by meddling in our affairs you will feel better. It is not down to you to roll up and be the heroes. It is for us, the real Nigerians, to save Nigeria. We do not need you! (*To* **Mama**.) Tell him, Mama.

She puts her hands out with the document.

Mama   Trust Kayode. He knows what he is doing.

Kunle *throws the papers out of her hands, sending them flying. He starts to cry.*

Kunle   I have been more than a son to you, I have done everything you have told me to do, *everything*, all this time. Mama, what have I been to you? . . .

Mama   My son please . . .

Kunle   TELL HIM TO RETURN BACK TO HIS COUNTRY NOW.

Silence.

Kunle   This man doesn't give a shit about you, Mama. I HAVE BEEN THE ONE THAT HAS BEEN THERE FOR YOU, CARED FOR YOU. I could have taken your money and run. I didn't need to stay around here for all this time. MAMA, TELL HIM TO LEAVE NOW.

Mama   I can't.

Silence.

Kunle   It seems you do have to share blood to be family. (*Pause.*) Truly thicker than water.

He exits.

Mama   Kunle wait . . .

Scene Ten

Nigeria. **Kayode** *is in the market place. He is handing out flyers alone. He is dressed in a suit, and the heat is slightly getting to him. The busy marketers ignore him as he hands out the flyers.* **Mama** *is helping out.*

Groundnut Trader   Groundnuts. Groundnuts. Ten naira Ten naira.

Pure Water Trader   Pure water, pure water.

Drinks Trader   Please, sa, buy Fanta.

He is approached by a **Beggar**.

Beggar   Oga, I beg make una give me ten naira. God go make you bigger.

Kayode   Wait a second.

He tries to address the busy **Traders** *but they walk past.*

Kayode   Hello, my name is . . .

He is pushed aside.

Pure Water Trader   Buy pure water!

Beggar   Oga, please!

Kayode   Excuse me a second, can I talk to you . . .

Mama   Talk to them in their language. This is a market. Sell them a product, Niaja-style, not British.

Kayode   I am not going to offer them money to . . .

Mama   Give our people more credit. It is not just money that people want.

Kayode *takes off his suit jacket and grabs a box. He stands on it and looks out at the traders who are still pacing up and down trying to sell produce.*

Pure Water Trader   Pure water, pure water, pure water, pure water.

Drinks Trader   Fanta, come and buy yogurt. One hundred naira. One twenty naira come and buy o.

Kayode   Ekasan, Ekale ejo ete eti e sile mo ni oro timofe bari e soro. [*Everyone listen up.*]

They stop.

Pure Water Trader   Ekasan . . .

Kayode   My name is Kayode Adetunji. I am running to be the new Councillor.

Pure Water Trader   Mr Hinglish eh so yoruba si wa now [*Mr English speak Yoruba to us.*]

Mama   Eh dake. [*Be silent.*] Listen to what he has to say.

Kayode *looks down at the crowd. He clears his throat and looks around nervously.*

Kayode (*in Yoruba*)   I am here to be the new Councillor of Ijebu-Ode.

Drinks Trader   Obama.

Kayode   No Obama ko. Kayode Adetunji ni mi o.

Beggar   What do you want?

Kayode   Tell me what you need.

They all speak at the same time.

Pure Water Trader   Owo. [*Money.*]

They all laugh.

Kayode   I am not here to offer money o.

*A **Trader** kisses his teeth and exits. **Traders** chat and lose interest.*

Kayode   Let me finish. I am here to talk to you because that Chief Olowolaye . . .

*The crowd boos at the sound of the **Chief**'s name.*

Kayode   He will run this town to the ground.

Pure Water Trader   We don tire jare!

Kayode   I am not going to stand here and lie to you and say I have struggled because I haven't . . . You need someone who is going to do something about all the issues . . .

*Some of the **Traders** get bored and walk off.*

Kayode   Like Obama did in America . . .

People hear the word Obama and they make their way back on stage.

I am here to offer you change.

Traders   Obama of Nigeria.

Beggar   Ema je kaso intoti oni she, eja so, ekoti oma she fuwa gho. [*Let's not talk about what you won't be doing. What will you be doing?*]

Kayode   Build better roads, improve transportation . . . more schools for children.

Groundnut Trader   We have school already jare.

Pure Water Trader   What are you going to do for awon agba? [*big people.*]

Beggar   It is not just the children that should get all the prizes.

Kayode   This town needs running water.

Groundnut Trader   We need light.

Beggar   Yes o.

Kayode   I am going to work on lighting the whole . . .

Groundnut Trader   This promise is nothing new. We just need cheaper generators.

Kayode   Generators are dangerous. We need constant electricity.

They cheer.

Do we not supply power to Ghana?

Groundnut Trader   We do o.

Kayode   So we can light somebody else's house but not our own.

Traders   It's true o!

Kayode (*in Yoruba*)   I am here to help light up Nigeria!

The crowd cheer.

Gege bi ewe iwoyi ani lati se awari asiwaju rere ya to si awon
aye deru olose lu ti won o mo se ileri fun wa pe awon o fun
wa ni ono ti o n yo kululu,omi ero to mon gara,ni bi awon
eleyi se se pataki to,won ko si ni je ki oro aje ori ilede Nijeria
go ke agba ni ogorun odun kan le logun si eyin. Ani ilo awon
asiwaju rere ti o je ki afi oju sun wa ati n ti okan wa fe,won o
si mu se. Aare ori lede ti o mu eto ilera ro run fun wa. Mo n
gbero la ti je ogbon ta gi olu di de ti o fe mu eto ilera ro run
fun wa ti ffo si je ko kari ile kari oko. Asiwaju to se tan la ti
gun le igbese ti o pe se ise fun ogun lo go odo ilu Nigerria.
Aare ti o fe la ti mu ite si waju ba awon agbe oko ni pa li lo
imo jinle ati eto ida si ara eni sile ti o fe fi ipin si iwa eleya me
yo ni pa oro epo la kan no.

Adari to ma ni igbagbo pe ori ilede Nigeria gbodo je ohun ti
won ma ka ye le wujo ori ilede agbaye,ti o si ma je ki ori ilede
yi go ke agba gege bi ori ilede to ti go ke agba.

[*As a new generation of Nigerians, we need to demand a new set of
leaders, not the bread-and-butter kind of politician, who will promise us
tarred roads and pipe-borne water − as important as these may be, they
are not going to make Nigeria a developed economy in the twenty-first
century. We need a new set of leaders who will inspire our hopes and stir
our hearts. A president who will finally make health care affordable . . .
I aim to be a worthy candidate who wants to make health care affordable
. . . and available to every single Nigerian, a leader willing to build a
system that will create millions of jobs for the average Nigerian, a
president . . . A leader who is willing to harness the ingenuity of farmers
and scientists and entrepreneurs to free this nation from the tyranny of oil
once and for all . . . A leader who believes Nigeria should be a force to be
reckoned with in the comity of nations and who is ready to lead us there.*]

Groundnut Trader   Obama, Obama.

Mama   Kayode!

Kayode   Kayode ni me o.

Everyone   Kayode, Kayode, Kayode.

The **Traders** *cheer and clap. They run over to* **Kayode** *and surround him.*

Mama (*singing*)   Baba ti se o. [*God has done it.*] Oti se o. [*He has done it.*]

Traders   Baba ti se o. [*God has done it.*] Oti se o. [*He has done it.*] Baba ti se o. [*God has done it.*] Olorun to wa bara le ru. [*God above that has made everything.*] Baba ti se o. [*God has done it.*]

Kayode *looks out at the crowd and smiles as they dance around him.*

Scene Eleven

Nigeria. **Chief Olowolaye** *is pacing up and down.* **Kunle** *watches him.*

Chief Olowolaye   That imbecile is out there running my name into the ground and . . . this was meant to be very easy. Now I have headache and all sort of nonsense. My doctor is telling me I am suffering stress. Why should I be suffering?

Kunle   Chief, please calm down . . .

Silence.

Chief Olowolaye   What are you going to do about this, Kunle?

Kunle   Me, sa?

Chief Olowolaye   No . . . me. Who else am I talking to?

Kunle   Sorry. I don't know what to –

Chief Olowolaye   This man is a problem and you need to fix it.

Kunle   He is doing this because he is angry with you.

Chief Olowolaye   How much does he want?

Kunle   He doesn't want money.

Chief Olowolaye   Everyone has a price.

Kunle   He doesn't . . . He . . . seems, erm . . .

Chief Olowolaye   Spill it out . . .

Kunle   He wants to change Nigeria.

Chief Olowolaye   That is the most stupid and uncommon-sense thing I have heard in all my life. This country does not need all these stupid people coming to Nigeria to take over.

Kunle   I know sa . . .

Chief Olowolaye   This is your problem, Kunle. You brought him to me . . . Deal with it.

Kunle   I don't know how.

Chief Olowolaye   If we do not win . . . you owe me 100 million.

Kunle   100 million?

Chief Olowolaye   I have commissioned contracts to suppliers . . .

Kunle   I thought there were only two contractors pre-approved . . .

Chief Olowolaye   All of them have been pre-approved and they will want their money.

Kunle   No no, sa. This is not what we agreed.

Chief Olowolaye   I will want my money, every penny I have invested in you.

Kunle   Sa, I cannot . . . I don't have that kind of money.

Chief Olowolaye   That stupid woman that is going around parading as your mother . . . go to her.

Kunle   Mama does not have that kind of money.

Chief Olowolaye   Are you stupid? Have you forgotten where you come from? Once a thief always a thief.

Kunle   I am no longer a thief, sa!

Chief Olowolaye *grabs* **Kunle** *by the throat.*

Chief Olowolaye   This was meant to be an easy race . . .
until that family . . . that man got involved.

Kunle *pushes* **Chief Olowolaye** *to the ground.*

Kunle   GET OFF ME! Who do you think you are, putting
your hands on me?

Kunle *grabs* **Chief Olowolaye***'s neck.*

Chief Olowolaye   You have lost all of your sense.

He is shocked, but the fire in **Kunle***'s eyes makes him react cautiously.*

Kunle   I have tried to be a gentleman. But you threaten my
life and think I am going to just bow down to you. NO. You
are not going to push me around any longer. You people with
money think you can pick and drop people any way you see
fit. Well, not me. I don't need Mama or you. Omo ita ni me.
[*I am a child of the streets.*] She gbo. [*Do you hear?*] Omo ita ni
me! E le she inkoko si me. Omo ita ni me. [*You can't do anything
to me I can't take. I am a child of the streets.*]

Chief Olowolaye *remains on the floor, scared. He doesn't move.*

Scene Twelve

Nigeria. **Kayode** *is in the living room, dressed in native wear for the
first time. He is pacing up and down the room looking at a piece of
paper. He stands still, holds the paper away from him and addresses*
Mama*, who is beaming from ear to ear.*

Kayode   As a nation, the time has come to move beyond
the distrust, bitterness, pettiness and anger that has consumed
our hearts for years. We need to end the political stranglehold
that has been all about division, and instead make it about
coalition – one that stretches through Northern states, Middle

belt, Western states and South states. As the new majority we are choosing hope over fear. We are choosing unity over division, and sending a powerful message that change is coming to Nigeria. It's time to stand up and tell those who think their money and their influence speak louder than our voices that they do not own this nation, we do. And we are here to take it back.

He reads the last line again with more emphasis and marks it on his piece of paper.

Mama   The speech is fantastic. And you look excellent!

Kayode   You think.

Mama   I know.

Buchi *enters the room with bags, followed by* **Rita** *and* **Fola**.

Buchi   Mama.

Kayode   Rita.

Mama   Where?

Rita   Hello.

Fola   Good evening, Ma.

She greets **Mama**.

Mama (*to* **Fola**)   Ah, my daughter! You are looking well!

Kayode   When did you get here?

He rushes over to her, but **Rita** *pushes him away.*

Rita (*to* **Mama**)   Hello.

Mama   Kayode, is this how your wife is going to greet – ?

Rita *realises her mistake and begs down.*

Rita   Sorry, I . . .

Mama *rolls her eyes.*

Rita   I got you a gift.

She takes out a duty-free bag and offers a perfume to **Mama** *with her left hand.* **Mama** *looks at the hand.*

Mama (*to* **Rita**)   I don't take things from people that give it with their left hands.

Rita   Fine.

Mama   And I have this one already.

Kayode   Fola, why didn't you call me?

Rita (*to* **Kayode**)   Can we talk in private?

Kayode (*to* **Mama**)   Can you excuse us, please, we need to –

Mama   You want me to leave my house so you can talk?

Kayode   Please . . .

Mama   And go where?

Kayode   To your room.

Mama   Ashakasha [*The cheek!*] But your friend is allowed to stay.

Kayode (*to* **Fola**)   Could you . . . ?

Fola   No problem. Make sure you tell your wife I had nothing to do with any of this. She hasn't been talking to me since duty-free.

Mama *exits with* **Fola**.

Kayode   She does it to wind you up.

Awkward silence.

Why didn't you tell me you were flying out?

Rita   Why is your picture plastered all over town?

Kayode   I have been calling you, left you messages. I called Fola too, and . . .

Rita   I thought she was telling me these things to wind me up . . . cos it has to be a joke, Kayode. It has to.

Kayode   I've got so much to fill you in on. Let's sit.

Rita   I'd rather stand.

Kayode   Please.

Rita   What are you wearing, Kayode?

Silence.

You leave me a series of crazy messages, don't return my phone calls.

Kayode   I have called you.

He stands awkwardly, looking at **Rita**. *She holds up a newspaper in her hand that has* **Kayode**'s *face with the words 'Africa Obama' splashed across the front page.*

Rita   What is this, Kayode?

He takes the newspaper.

The new African Obama!

Kayode   I am not trying to be President.

Rita   You're running for local government! Your clothes –

Kayode (*looking down at his clothes*)   My mother made it for me. Why didn't you tell me you were coming out here?

Rita   I CALLED YOU BACK!

Kayode   When?

Rita   I've left messages with your mother and . . .

Kayode   She didn't give them to me.

Rita   Of course.

Kayode   Take a seat.

Rita   I'd rather stand!

Pause.

What have you been doing here, Kayode? If this is a joke, a way for you and Fola to get me over here, you can say it now. It worked, after twenty years, I'm here. So ha ha.

Kayode   It's not a joke. I've been working on a campaign.

Rita *begins to shake her head and sinks into the chair.*

Rita   Do you know how it feels to find out that my husband is . . . didn't think I needed to know, before you made such a drastic decision you didn't think you needed to run it past me first?

Kayode   I called you.

Rita   And what if I said no? . . . Have you forgotten I'm your wife? . . . Life-changing decisions should be made jointly. I feel like I have been living a lie.

Kayode   Rita, I wanted to surprise you.

Rita   A SURPRISE, KAYODE, A SURPRISE IS TAKING ME TO PARIS, NOT THIS . . .

Kayode   Keep your voice down.

Rita   No, I won't keep my voice down.

Kayode   It is not as bad as you think.

Rita   Why? Why am I the last to know? Why hide it?

Kayode   I'm not hiding anything.

Mama *enters.*

Mama   Is everything okay?

Kayode   Mum, please give us a bit of privacy.

Mama   I don't like shouting in my house.

Kayode   Please. I am trying to talk to my wife.

Mama *exits.*

Rita   Just a holiday . . . just going to rest. You failed to tell me you are in this country running in an election.

Kayode I did call you. You haven't even told me what you were up to back there.

Rita Don't you dare make this about me. This is all about you. You are living another life!

Kayode I am not.

Rita Yes, you are!

Kayode I am doing this for us, Rita.

She shakes her head.

Rita What 'us'? 'Us' is London, our mortgage, our flat . . . our home. 'Us' is definitely not what you are doing here. This thing, that is all you. You and you alone. You selfish piece of shit, Kayode.

Pause.

I don't know you any more.

Kayode Course you do . . .

Rita YOU TURN YOUR BACK ON EVERYTHING, EVERYONE. THAT'S NOT THE KAYODE I KNOW. WHAT ARE YOU WEARING?

Kayode *takes off his 'agbada' and hat, leaving him in his vest and trousers.*

Rita Fola and your mother must be laughing up there.

Pause.

I've supported everything you have ever done.

Silence.

Since I have met you, I have been there for you. I've sacrificed. Done everything . . . You said you needed a break, a holiday and instead . . .

Kayode I got carried away, okay. I –

Rita   YOU ARE RUNNING IN AN ELECTION. That is not what I would call 'getting carried away'.

Kayode   It all happened so fast . . . they were telling me I don't belong here.

Rita   So? You don't!

Kayode   I had to show them, needed to prove to them . . .

Rita   What? Everything is a game to you.

Kayode   That's not true. I'm good at what I do. I can actually make a difference here, Rita. I can do this. Please, honey, believe me this is not a game. I can do this. I'm actually in with a chance of winning and not because anyone feels pity for me or feels they need 'to give the black one a chance'. For the first time in my life I'm not reminded that I'm black. You can't begin to imagine what that feels like, to be that free. To be special but not special because I am black. Special because I'm good . . .

Rita   Are we over?

Kayode   No.

Rita   Then what? . . . How are you going to run your office from London? . . . Or do you plan on relocating here?

Silence.

Is this a mid-life crisis?

Kayode   No.

Silence.

Baby, I am sorry, okay . . . I felt that spark again. The same spark . . . The early days . . . before everything else. I am consumed by that spark again. The need to change the world, that yearning for something better. I got it back, baby.

Rita   Is this your life now? The new Obama?

Kayode   I don't know.

Mama *enters the room again, followed by a sheepish* **Fola**.

Mama   I am sorry to interrupt, but we have to work on your speech for the . . .

Kayode   Can it not wait? I need to speak to −

Mama   It cannot.

Rita *moves as if to leave.*

Fola   Where are you going?

Rita   I'm still not talking to you!

Fola   Kayode, tell her I knew nothing about this!

Rita   I just need to −

Mama   I can get a driver to take her to her hotel . . .

Kayode   She is not going to a hotel. She is staying here.

Rita   I can't stay here.

Mama   We shouldn't force her to stay.

Rita *tries to leave.*

Fola   Rita! Where can you go?

Mama   Let her go!

Rita   How is it even possible for you to run . . . don't even live here?

Fola   The rules are slightly flexible here.

Rita *gives* **Fola** *a dirty look.*

Kayode   Can you leave us to sort things out please?

Mama   I am not going in and out of the room. If you people want to continue this conversation you can −

Rita   This isn't your home.

Mama   It is o.

Kayode   Please hear me out.

Rita   Never satisfied with the life you have. Always looking for something else to make you happy. I have sacrificed my life . . .

Kayode   We both agreed that . . .

Rita   WRONG AGAIN. Are you coming home?

Mama   HE IS HOME

Rita   I'M TALKING TO MY HUSBAND! Answer the question, Kayode?

Kayode   I . . .

Buchi (*offstage*)   MAMA! MAMA!

Buchi *brings in* **Kunle**, *who is dripping with blood.* **Fola** *and* **Rita** *scream and edge away from the door.*

Buchi   MAMA!

Kayode   What happened? (*To* **Buchi**.) Call an ambulance!

Mama   No. Bring the car!

Rita   What is going on?

Mama *runs over to* **Kunle**.

Mama   KUNLE. Egbami o.

Fola   What happened?

Rita (*to* **Kayode**)   Who is he?

Mama   Kunle kilo she o. [*What happened?*] Olrun egba mi o.

Kunle *is in agony.*

Mama   Kunle o. Omo mi please . . .

Kunle   OMO ITA NI . . .

He coughs up blood as he struggles to get his words out.

Kunle   Ori ilede Nigeria ti ba je! [*It's your fault Nigeria is spoilt.*]

Fola *comes in and tries to stop the bleeding.*

Mama   No, Kunle . . . no . . . no no.

Rita   Someone call the police.

Mama   KUNLE! We have to get him to the hospital.

Rita   You can't move him. Wait for the ambulance.

Fola   They won't come. Kayode!

Mama (*to* **Kayode**)   Help me carry him.

Kayode *is in shock.* **Fola** *tries to help pick up* **Kunle** *with* **Mama**. *They struggle to carry him.* **Mama** *cries.*

Fola   KAYODE.

Kayode   This is all my fault.

Kunle *flops over.*

Mama   KUNLE!

She starts to cry and buries herself on **Kunle**. **Fola** *and* **Buchi** *back away.*

Mama   Kunle jo wo da ri gin mi omo mi ki ni mo se o. [*Please forgive me, my son. What have I done?*]

(*To* **Kayode**.) CAN YOU STOP STANDING THERE AND HELP?

Kayode *shakes his head.*

Blackout.

Methuen Drama Modern Plays

include work by

Edward Albee

Jean Anouilh

John Arden

Margaretta D'Arcy

Peter Barnes

Sebastian Barry

Brendan Behan

Dermot Bolger

Edward Bond

Bertolt Brecht

Howard Brenton

Anthony Burgess

Simon Burke

Jim Cartwright

Caryl Churchill

Complicite

Noël Coward

Lucinda Coxon

Sarah Daniels

Nick Darke

Nick Dear

Shelagh Delaney

David Edgar

David Eldridge

Dario Fo

Michael Frayn

John Godber

Paul Godfrey

David Greig

John Guare

Peter Handke

David Harrower

Jonathan Harvey

Iain Heggie

Declan Hughes

Terry Johnson

Sarah Kane

Charlotte Keatley

Barrie Keeffe

Howard Korder

Robert Lepage

Doug Lucie

Martin McDonagh

John McGrath

Terrence McNally

David Mamet

Patrick Marber

Arthur Miller

Mtwa, Ngema & Simon

Tom Murphy

Phyllis Nagy

Peter Nichols

Sean O'Brien

Joseph O'Connor

Joe Orton

Louise Page

Joe Penhall

Luigi Pirandello

Stephen Poliakoff

Franca Rame

Mark Ravenhill

Philip Ridley

Reginald Rose

Willy Russell

Jean-Paul Sartre

Sam Shepard

Wole Soyinka

Simon Stephens

Shelagh Stephenson

Peter Straughan

C. P. Taylor

Theatre Workshop

Sue Townsend

Judy Upton

Timberlake Wertenbaker

Roy Williams

Snoo Wilson

Victoria Wood

Methuen Drama Contemporary Dramatists

include

John Arden (two volumes)
Arden & D'Arcy
Peter Barnes (three volumes)
Sebastian Barry
Dermot Bolger
Edward Bond (eight volumes)
Howard Brenton
  (two volumes)
Richard Cameron
Jim Cartwright
Caryl Churchill (two volumes)
Sarah Daniels (two volumes)
Nick Darke
David Edgar (three volumes)
David Eldridge
Ben Elton
Dario Fo (two volumes)
Michael Frayn (three volumes)
David Greig
John Godber (four volumes)
Paul Godfrey
John Guare
Lee Hall (two volumes)
Peter Handke
Jonathan Harvey
  (two volumes)
Declan Hughes
Terry Johnson (three volumes)
Sarah Kane
Barrie Keeffe
Bernard-Marie Koltès
  (two volumes)
Franz Xaver Kroetz
David Lan
Bryony Lavery
Deborah Levy
Doug Lucie

David Mamet (four volumes)
Martin McDonagh
Duncan McLean
Anthony Minghella
  (two volumes)
Tom Murphy (six volumes)
Phyllis Nagy
Anthony Neilsen (two volumes)
Philip Osment
Gary Owen
Louise Page
Stewart Parker (two volumes)
Joe Penhall (two volumes)
Stephen Poliakoff
  (three volumes)
David Rabe (two volumes)
Mark Ravenhill (two volumes)
Christina Reid
Philip Ridley
Willy Russell
Eric-Emmanuel Schmitt
Ntozake Shange
Sam Shepard (two volumes)
Wole Soyinka (two volumes)
Simon Stephens (two volumes)
Shelagh Stephenson
David Storey (three volumes)
Sue Townsend
Judy Upton
Michel Vinaver
  (two volumes)
Arnold Wesker (two volumes)
Michael Wilcox
Roy Williams (three volumes)
Snoo Wilson (two volumes)
David Wood (two volumes)
Victoria Wood

Methuen Drama Student Editions

Jean Anouilh *Antigone* • John Arden *Serjeant Musgrave's Dance*
Alan Ayckbourn *Confusions* • Aphra Behn *The Rover* • Edward Bond
Lear • *Saved* • Bertolt Brecht *The Caucasian Chalk Circle* • *Fear and
Misery in the Third Reich* • *The Good Person of Szechwan* • *Life of Galileo* •
Mother Courage and her Children • *The Resistible Rise of Arturo Ui* • *The
Threepenny Opera* • Anton Chekhov *The Cherry Orchard* • *The Seagull* •
Three Sisters • *Uncle Vanya* • Caryl Churchill *Serious Money* • *Top Girls*
• Shelagh Delaney *A Taste of Honey* • Euripides *Elektra* • *Medea* •
Dario Fo *Accidental Death of an Anarchist* • Michael Frayn *Copenhagen*
• John Galsworthy *Strife* • Nikolai Gogol *The Government Inspector* •
Robert Holman *Across Oka* • Henrik Ibsen *A Doll's House* • *Ghosts* •
Hedda Gabler • Charlotte Keatley *My Mother Said I Never Should* •
Bernard Kops *Dreams of Anne Frank* • Federico García Lorca *Blood
Wedding* • *Doña Rosita the Spinster* (bilingual edition) • *The House of
Bernarda Alba* • (bilingual edition) • *Yerma* (bilingual edition) • David
Mamet *Glengarry Glen Ross* • *Oleanna* • Patrick Marber *Closer* • John
Marston *Malcontent* • Martin McDonagh *The Lieutenant of Inishmore* •
Joe Orton *Loot* • Luigi Pirandello *Six Characters in Search of an Author*
• Mark Ravenhill *Shopping and F***ing* • Willy Russell *Blood Brothers*
• *Educating Rita* • Sophocles *Antigone* • *Oedipus the King* • Wole
Soyinka *Death and the King's Horseman* • Shelagh Stephenson *The
Memory of Water* • August Strindberg *Miss Julie* • J. M. Synge *The
Playboy of the Western World* • Theatre Workshop *Oh What a Lovely
War* Timberlake Wertenbaker *Our Country's Good* • Arnold Wesker
The Merchant • Oscar Wilde *The Importance of Being Earnest* •
Tennessee Williams *A Streetcar Named Desire* • *The Glass Menagerie*

For a complete catalogue of Methuen Drama titles
write to:

Methuen Drama
50 Bedford Square
London
WC1B 3DP

or you can visit our website at:

www.methuendrama.com